BOSTON SYMPHONY

CHARLES MUNCH, Conductor

Wednesday, May 20 8:30 P.M.

"School for Scandal" Barber
Symphony No. 2 for Strings Honegger
Symphony No. 5 Ravel
Brahms

NOW $2.75 - $3.75 - $4.70

MASSEY HALL

MART KENNEY'S RANCH
DANCING TONIGHT
and Saturday
BOYD VALLEAU AND HIS ORCHESTRA

Admission 1.50 per person — For Reservations, RA. 6102

★ COMPLETE PICNIC FACILITIES AVAILABLE

DUFFERIN DRIVE-IN THEATRE

SHOWING TONIGHT
JUDY HOLLIDAY
ALDO RAY
The Marrying Kind
— Cartoon - Short - News
MIDNIGHT SHOW
SUNDAY

CHILDREN UNDER 12 YEARS Free

JAZZ FESTIVAL

DIZZY   CHARLIE PARKER
BUD POWELL   MINGUS
Plus CBC

TONIGHT AT 8.30 P.M.

Tickets Now at All Agencies and Premier Radio

ROYAL ALEXANDRA
HOUSE OF UNIVERSITY AVE.

NIGHT (8:20)

GOOD NITE LADIES

CHRISTOPHER FRY'S

THE LADY'S NOT FOR BURNING

Tonight 8.30

HOUSE THEATRE

The wonderful story of a wish come true!
Irene Dunne
with DEAN JAGGER
"IT GROWS ON TREES"

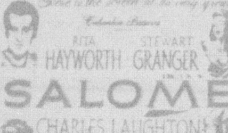

Columbia Pictures
RITA HAYWORTH   STEWART GRANGER
in
SALOME
CHARLES LAUGHTON

DANFORTH ★ FAIRLAWN ★ HUMBER

COOL BLUES

COOL BLUES

Charlie Parker in Canada 1953

Mark Miller

Nightwood Editions
London, Ontario

Published in Canada by Nightwood Editions, Box 1426, Station A,
London, Ontario N6A 5M2.
(Nightwood Editions is a division of blewointmentpress ltd.)

This book has been published with the assistance of the block grant
programs of the Canada Council and the Ontario Arts Council.

Typeset by Imprint Typesetting, Toronto. Design and layout by
Maureen Cochrane and David Lee. Printed in Canada by Gagné.

Canadian Cataloguing in Publication Data

Miller, Mark, 1951-
        Cool Blues : Charlie Parker in Canada 1953

ISBN 0-88971-119-4

1. Parker, Charlie, 1920-1955 - Influence.
2. Jazz music - Canada - History and criticism.
I. Title.

ML419.P4M54 1989   788'.66'0924   C89-094873-9

Contents

1. Preface 7

2. Acknowledgements 11

3. Introduction: Bird *Lived* 15

4. Prologue: The White Plastic Alto 20

5. The Jazz Workshop, Montreal 23

6. Massey Hall, Toronto 55

7. Epilogue (I) 97

8. Epilogue (II) 99

9. Discography 101

10. Bibliography 107

11. Index 110

Preface

The central figure of *Cool Blues* is Charlie Parker. The story of *Cool Blues*, however, is more than the story of any one person.

Cool Blues is about the presence of one man, a musician of considerable legend, in two specific places at two specific times. It is no less about those places, Montreal and Toronto, at those times, February and May of 1953.

It is, then, in small part biography and in larger part history – at that, social history as well as jazz history.

Its perspective is split. It is about two events, Parker's performances on CBC TV and at the Chez Paree in Montreal at the instigation of that city's Jazz Workshop, and his Massey Hall appearance with Dizzy Gillespie, Bud Powell, Charles Mingus and Max Roach in Toronto under the sponsorship of the New Jazz Society.

It is also about the ways in which those events have been remembered. It is about the things that Parker and the musicians with him are known to have done; it is also about the things they were seen to do – from somewhat closer at hand in Montreal than in Toronto.

The Jazz Workshop performances remain relatively obscure in the annals of Parker biography, although they hold a certain significance in the history of jazz in Montreal. The Toronto concert, on the other hand, is one the most famous events in the music's first 90-odd years and has made Massey Hall second only to Oscar Peterson among the most recognizable Canadian names in jazz.

It is in this spirit that I have undertaken *Cool Blues*. These are *Canadian* stories, no matter that many of the principals involved, Charlie Parker first and foremost, are American. Indeed, so much of the history of jazz in Canada involves American musicians in either direct or indirect roles, as full participants or distant models. This is simply another example, in some fleeting way a study of the relationship between Canadians and Americans − of the former's self-conscious deference and the latter's indomitable influence.

The incidents described in *Cool Blues* took place 36 years ago. For Charlie Parker, 36 years represents more than a lifetime.

For the surviving participants, 36 years is simply a long time − a long time to remember the specifics of his three nights in Montreal and his single night in Toronto. Indeed, it is more than enough time to forget.

Any attempt to reconstruct Parker's Jazz Workshop and Massey Hall appearances nevertheless depends on the memories of those who were present − fellow musicians, organizers and fans alike, each of whom have a slightly different angle on the particular event.

Of course, several of the major figures have died − Parker, most significantly, as well as Harold (Steep) Wade, Brew Moore and Bob Rudd, who participated in the Jazz Workshop performances, and Charles Mingus, Bud Powell and many of the Toronto musicians who were involved in the Massey Hall concert.

Others have proven elusive − Dick Garcia and Valdo Williams, for example, again from the Jazz Workshop. Others still remain active but have recollections that seem confused, either by time or self-interest. Moreover, some of those participants who bore first-hand witness to either the Jazz Workshop or Massey Hall events have since become familiar with second-hand accounts. The resulting, undifferentiated "reminiscences" mix the two freely, perpetuating second-hand fallacy and fabrication as first-hand fact.

I have in these cases exercised my own judgement, building a narrative of recollection on the framework of what little retrievable information remains from 1953 − for the most part, newspaper accounts of the day.

Naturally, smaller and larger contradictions abound. New information, re-discovered fact or plain logic call into question the time-honored version of various incidents; the recollections of different witnesses to the same incident fail to agree; the recollections of a single witness change with the passing of years.

Here, too, I have exercised my own judgement where it seems reasonable to do so. Elsewhere, I have simply presented the contradictory accounts and invite the reader to marvel at the caprice of the human memory.

The initial documentation of these events remains the most important: the music that Parker played on both occasions, including two versions of the tune that gives this book its title, was recorded – not quite *all* of the music in either case, but more than enough to ensure both a place of honor in the Parker story.

Various accounts of the Massey Hall concert have been published. Among them: Bill Coss' liner notes to the original Debut release of performances from the concert, and those of Stephen Davis to the later Prestige reissue; passages in biographies of Parker (by Ross Russell and Brian Priestley), Dizzy Gillespie (by Gillespie himself and Barry McRae) and Charles Mingus (by Priestley again); entries in various discographies, including Jack Litchfield's *The Canadian Jazz Discography 1916-1980*. (Full citations follow in the bibliography, p. 107.)

The Priestley books and the Litchfield discography seem most reliable in retrospect; the Davis notes, and their acknowledged source, the Russell bio, least. (Russell's unacknowledged source, ironically, appears to be letters published in *Jazz Journal* from two Toronto journalists present at the concert.)

On the other hand, little has been written about Parker's appearance in Montreal. The few references to date are generally of a discographical nature, and some of those are clearly based solely on the aural evidence provided by surviving tapes of the performances. (Thus, among Parker's accompanists, Neil Michaud becomes Neil "Michel" and Ted Paskert is Ted "Pastor" in some entries.) Again, the Litchfield discography clearly holds the most authority.

Paul Bley has also spoken on occasion of Parker's Jazz Workshop performances. He was quoted by Len Lyons in *Contemporary Keyboard* (May 1977) as saying: "I hired Charlie Parker to play with me, and I did that by learning to make transactions early. I was 16. He was in a basement in New York. I lived in a suburb of Montreal. So I got on a plane, went to New York, took him by the hand, and led him to Montreal." In fact, Bley was 20. In fact, Bley is remembered by other musicians to have preceded Parker to Montreal.

A second Bley account, from 1984, appears in my book *Boogie, Pete & the Senator.*

Magazine or newspaper pieces have been published on or close to the anniversaries of both events by journalists in the respective cities, Len Dobbin in Montreal and Peter Goddard, Jack Batten and myself in Toronto. (Again, citations follow in the bibliography.)

Dobbin, in fact, was present for the Jazz Workshop events 36 years ago, as was Batten at Massey Hall.

I was present at neither.

I came to know of the Massey Hall concert in the same way that jazz fans the world around have known about it – from the recordings. I was pleased to know that an event trumpeted as "The Greatest Jazz Concert Ever" had taken place in Toronto.

I was curious to know how and why.

I would learn later of Parker's Jazz Workshop performances from vague, passing references in the legend and lore of jazz in Montreal.

I was curious to know more.

Cool Blues is the product of that curiosity.

Acknowledgements

Cool Blues has been prepared from interviews done by the author between May of 1988 and July of 1989. Unless otherwise indicated, all quoted material is taken from these sources.

I am indebted to the many people who took the time to recreate the events described in *Cool Blues*. They are listed here with my appreciation.

At the Jazz Workshop (Montreal): Carlton Baird, Paul Bley, Don Cameron, Len Dobbin, Gordie Fleming, Hal Gaylor, Bill Graham, Buddy Jordan, Bert Joss, Yvan Landry, Jean (John) Lymburner, B.T. Lundy, Bobby Malloy, Neil Michaud, Huguette (Rajotte) Schwartz, Art Roberts, Bob Roby, Abby Smollen, Vic Vogel, Alfie Wade, Keith White and Wilkie Wilkinson...

At Massey Hall (Toronto): Alex Barris, Jack Batten, Len Boyd, Don Brown, Gary and Marg Dutton, Gordie Evans, Roger Feather, Julian Filanowski, Ralph Fraser, Dizzy Gillespie, Oscar Goodstein, Art Granatstein, Jim Harper, Bill Hoare, Helen McNamara, Eugene Miller, Howie Morris, Boyd Raeburn, Steve Richards, Max Roach, Alan Scharf, Norman Symonds, Erich Traugott, Dick Wattam, Hart Wheeler and Celia Zaentz.

Several people assisted my efforts to locate participants in the Jazz Workshop and Massey Hall episodes, supplied background information or extended various professional and personal courtesies. These include Bob Bregman, Ross Brethour, Warren Chiasson, Gene DiNovi, Len Dobbin, Fred Duligal, Barry Elmes, Heidi Fleming, John Gilmore, Hal Hill, Moe Koffman, Pat LaBarbera, Alastair Lawrie, Peter Leitch, Judith McErvel, John Norris, Brian Priestley, Joe Puma, George Shearing, Bill Smith, Royce Speight, Dr. Billy Taylor, Don Thompson, Fred Topping, Sherrie Tucker, Patricia Wardrop, Chuck Wayne, Hart Wheeler, Keith White and Kevin Whitehead. I thank them all.

My thanks also...

To Mrs. Mary Robinson of Toronto, for the use of her late husband's photographs from the Massey Hall concert. I am honored to present them in *Cool Blues*, some for the first time, and I am pleased to give Harold Robinson the photo credit that almost invariably has been missing on the occasions when the others have been published...

To Alan Scharf of Saskatoon and Huguette Schwartz of Montreal, for allowing me to use their photographs from Massey Hall and the Chez Paree respectively.

To Dennis Robinson, for the prints of his father's photographs and for the copy negative of the Schwartz photo; to Paul Hoeffler for copy negatives of the Scharf photos...

To Keith White and André White, for the complete tape of Parker's Montreal performances; to Jack Litchfield, for the complete tape of CBFT's "Jazz Workshop," including the performances *without* Parker; to Hart Wheeler, for the tape of the "CBC All-Stars" at Massey Hall; to Ted O'Reilly, of CJRT-FM (Toronto), for taped excerpts from his interview in 1975 with Charles Mingus...

To Keith White again, for access to his unpublished memoir, *Noting the Scene*, and for copies of his transcriptions of Parker's Montreal solos...

And to Jack Batten, David Lancashire, David Lee, Jack Litchfield, Huguette Schwartz and Sherrie Tucker for their editorial comments, suggestions and corrections.

I also offer my appreciation to Bob Bregman, Marc-André Chenard, Lucinda Chodan, Monika Croydon, Peter Danson, Len Dobbin, John Gilmore, Raymond Gervais, Bill Grove, Marie-Lynn Hammond, Paul Hoeffler, David Lancashire, Andrea LeBorgne, Jack Litchfield, Ruth Miller, Victoria Sanderson, Alan Scharf,

Sherrie Tucker, Carole Warren and Kevin Whitehead, all of whom have encouraged the work on *Cool Blues* in various ways and at various times.

Finally, I must thank David Lee and Maureen Cochrane of Nightwood Editions for their immediate interest in the original idea for this book, for their ongoing support of my efforts to document the history of jazz in Canada, and for their care and concern in seeing *Cool Blues* into print.

*

The research and writing of *Cool Blues* was assisted by a grant from the Writers' Reserve of the Ontario Arts Council in 1988.

Mark Miller
August 1989

Introduction: Bird *Lived*

The paint has not faded in the hot sun of the Canadian summer. The message is clear – just two words scrawled on the west wall of a corner building at Clark and Prince Arthur in a residential neighbourhood of downtown Montreal.

BIRD LIVES

Other slogans dashed against nearby walls speak in defiance, or in anger, of life in this island city during the late 1980s. Some hail Bill 101, asserting the primacy of the French language in Quebec. Others are racist. Still others, anti-semitic.

BIRD LIVES, however, sounds a celebratory note, one that has echoed down through the years since the same two words first appeared on Greenwich Village walls in the days following Charlie Parker's death on March 12, 1955.

Charles Parker, Jr. – Bird – spent much of his short life challenging his own mortality. Even if he made it only into the seventh month of his 35th year, he seems to have beaten the odds magnificently.

He started early, already a professional musician, a husband, a father and a drug user, if not a drug addict, in his teens. By then, Parker wasn't long for Kansas City. He had been born in the town across the Kaw river in Kansas on August 29, 1920, but raised in the big city on the Missouri side – raised mostly, and adoringly, by his

mother Addie in the absence of his father. Charles Sr. was an alco-
holic whose slow demise saw him fall from the TOBA vaudeville
circuit as a singer and dancer to the Pullman rail line as a chef
before he was slashed to death in 1939 by a prostitute.

Charles Jr. would have to return from New York to Kansas City
to bury his father. Still nominally a teenager, he had already developed, if not fully realized, the extended harmonic comprehension
and the extraordinary technical virtuosity that would shake jazz to
its foundations once his early recordings with Tiny Grimes (for Savoy
in 1944) and with Dizzy Gillespie (for Guild in 1945) were heard.

Parker had matured quickly.

At 16, he was the target of a cymbal flung in disgust by drummer
Jo Jones at a Kansas City jam session; responding to Jones' dis-
missal, he hawked all the more closely older KC musicians, among
them tenorman Tommy Douglas, altoist Buster Smith, guitarist
Efferge Ware and pianist Carrie Powell.

At 18 he washed dishes in the back of a Harlem chicken joint
while Art Tatum dazzled at the piano out front with his harmonic
reconstructions, his quotes from pop-song literature and his double-
time virtuosity.

At 19, still in a back room – this time at a Seventh Avenue chili
house with guitarist Biddy Fleet – Parker established his own harmonic groundwork, on which he, Dizzy, Thelonious Monk and a
few others would build the towering music called bebop in the next
few years.

Meanwhile, the salacious side of Parker's life was off to an equally fast start and would only become more salacious over the years.
His appetite for heroin, alcohol, food and sex was, in turn, vora-
cious, legendary and, finally, consuming.

He was in many ways a scoundrel, though an exceedingly charming scoundrel, as he went about his ways and means of meeting his
immediate needs. Any less gifted a musician would surely not have
been indulged by friends, fans and fellow jazzmen to the extent that
Parker was – and Parker was only the most gifted musician of his
generation. In every respect, he was an imposing figure.

The complications of his youth, taken together with his self-
developed genius and his place as a black musician at the forefront

of a musical revolution in a white America, may only begin to explain fully the convolutions of his adult life, prematurely attained as it was. Nevertheless, they surely portend that there would indeed be convolutions. No one from such a background could be expected to lead an unremarkable life. In Parker's case the surprise may be that he led any life at all, let alone one – in strictly musical terms – so productive.

Parker returned to New York in 1942. After a few years more with big bands – the bluesy Jay McShann orchestra, with which he arrived, and the more sophisticated Earl Hines and Billy Eckstine bands, with which he again left briefly – Parker, too, moved out front.

The back rooms were thereafter reserved for his other obsessions.

Now in his early twenties, he was already into the second half of his life, the best of years and the worst of years. His renown in the jazz community – his fame to his acolytes and sycophants, his noto-riety to his detractors – grew quickly. He was billed as "America's outstanding jazz solo saxophonist" when he appeared with trom-bonist Trummy Young, pianist Erroll Garner, bassist Slam Stewart and drummer Harold (Doc) West at Massey Hall in Toronto on November 14, 1945, two weeks *before* he had made his first records under his own name for Savoy. (Not for the last time, a reviewer from *The Globe and Mail* made rather more fuss of the pianist in the band at Massey Hall than of Parker; the concert was surely Bird's first advertised appearance in Canada, although he may have crossed the border previously as a member of the Hines or McShann bands.)

Yet, within nine months Parker was committed to Camarillo State Hospital, a California mental health centre. Provided, in effect, with a fresh start, he gained his freedom early in 1947 and soon undertook an historic, year-long series of recordings for Savoy and Dial that stand with the finest in jazz history.

Old habits die hard, however, and the final eight years of Parker's life must often have seemed like a rollercoaster ride through the darkest of nights. Only his music, created with some sort of sixth sense that may have been nothing more than an indomitable instinct for survival, kept him on track at all.

There were new settings for the Parker alto – Machito's Latin orchestra in 1948, for example, and a small string ensemble in 1949. The latter's recordings of *April in Paris* and *Just Friends* proved popular enough that Parker would perform in clubs and in concert with the formation.

In triumph, he travelled to France in 1949 and toured Scandinavia briefly in 1950; in need, he also took work where he could get it, and with whatever sidemen were available, be they practiced New York freelancers or awed, inexperienced locals.

It was apparently in need that Parker came to Canada in February of 1953 to appear on television and at the Chez Paree in Montreal, but it would surely have been in triumph that he returned three months later to perform again at Massey Hall in Toronto, this time with Dizzy Gillespie, Bud Powell, Charles Mingus and Max Roach.

He was recorded on both occasions – semi-officially in Toronto and unofficially in Montreal – as he was, or so it seems in retrospect, in most of his later appearances. Gathered together by various discographers, these amateur recordings and authorized or unauthorized airchecks provide an approximate itinerary for his last years. In the three months between the Canadian concerts, he did several broadcasts from both the Bandbox and Birdland in New York and at least one from Storyville in Boston, and he made one appearance at the Kavakos Grill and two at the Howard Theatre in Washington.

Parker was playing well in this period. The Massey Hall recording ranks with the most important of his career, while the Kavakos and Storyville sets (issued respectively as *One Night in Washington*, Elektra Musician XE1-60019, in 1982 and *Bird at Storyville*, Blue Note BT 85108, in 1988), as well as the anthologized performances from Montreal (see Discography, p. 101) show him in commanding form. He remained a vibrant and often inspired presence despite the informality and uncertainties of the particular engagement and the routine of a small, now oft-repeated repertoire of original tunes and popular standards.

Indeed, the vigour of his playing belies his personal anguish early in 1953. For one, his daughter Pree was ill. "My baby girl is a city case in the hospital because her health has been neglected since we hadn't the necessary doctor fees," Parker wrote on February 17 to the State Liquor Authority in a letter concerning the status of his cabaret card, the permit needed to work in New York nightclubs.

For another, his own health was in decline. He had ulcers. A heart condition had been detected. The cirrhosis of his liver was underway, and its effects were no doubt starting to be felt.

Pree would live only a year more. Parker, just two.

The mythology of Charlie Parker was already in place when BIRD LIVES began to appear on New York walls in mid-March of 1955. The mythology had grown beyond all reasonable proportion when the same words were painted on a wall of a corner building a dozen blocks from the Chez Paree in downtown Montreal.

BIRD LIVES... The very words trap Charlie Parker in the perpetual present.

But Charlie Parker lived.

Bird *lived*.

Prologue: The White Plastic Alto

I'm as happy as a Bird with my King Super 20

– Charlie Parker, advertisement,
Metronome March 1953

A smiling Charlie Parker may have endorsed King saxophones early in 1953, but he was playing a white, acrylic Grafton alto in Montreal in February, at Massey Hall in May, and on at least two other documented occasions in between, once with The Orchestra at Washington's Kavakos Grill and once on a New York radio broadcast during which the emcee makes a point of asking about the instrument. Max Roach also remembers Parker playing the horn around New York during this period; the Grafton was still in Parker's possession at the time of his death two years later.

Thus, the suggestion (advanced by Ross Russell in *Bird Lives!*, apparently on the basis of a letter published in the May 1970 issue of *Jazz Journal*) that Parker arrived for the Massey Hall concert without an instrument and borrowed the Grafton from a local music store at the last minute seems improbable.

Such a story may well have its origins simply in the need to account for Parker's use of a saxophone that had the appearance of being little more than a novelty. (The Grafton was in fact a legitimate instrument, introduced in Britain during the post-war years when brass was scarce.) Furthermore, apart from Harold Robinson's famous Massey Hall photographs, there have been few, if any, pictures published of Parker playing the white horn, which might lead to the conclusion that he in fact used it on just this one occasion.

The Jazz Workshop

The winter of 1952-3 was one of Montreal's mildest in years. The snow had already started to disappear from downtown streets in early February; the dark, slickened pavement shone with the bright lights of store displays along *rue* Ste-Catherine and glowed under the nightclub marquees and softly-lit restaurant windows up and down cross streets with good British names like Peel, Stanley, Drummond and Bishop.

Headlines on the 5th, the day of Charlie Parker's arrival in Montreal, noted the annual flooding in the city's south-shore communities of Longueuil and Ville Jacques Cartier as temperatures hovered around the freezing mark and pack ice began to jam the St. Lawrence River.

It was a fairly routine week for news in Montreal – the Union Nationale party announced a new provincial budget, Mayor Camillien Houde celebrated his 30th year in politics and the Canadiens were reported to have signed Quebec amateur hockey sensation Jean Beliveau to a professional contract – but it would be, if only in retrospect, an altogether remarkable week for music. Louis Armstrong had closed an engagement at the Seville Theatre on Wednesday, the 4th. Frank Sinatra would open a 10-night stand at the Chez Paree on the 6th. The concert violinist Yehudi Menuhin had come and gone to great acclaim at Her Majesty's Theatre on the 3rd.

Charlie Parker would come on the 5th and go on the 7th to very little notice at all just another bulky figure on Montreal's glistening downtown streets.

Still 20 months away from the headlines, a judicial commission headed by Mr. Justice François Caron and prosecuted by lawyers Pacifique (Pax) Plante and Jean Drapeau continued its investigation into vice and corruption in Montreal from 1940 to 1950.

One career was made by the inquiry – Drapeau immediately announced his candidacy for mayor and swept into power just 18 days after the commission's damning, 100,000-word report was made public in October of 1954. Many other careers suffered, in particular those of the city's nightclub performers, jazz musicians among them, who were thrown out of work by Drapeau's subsequent vigilance against organized crime.

Montreal of the early 1950s was not necessarily a great town for jazz. It was, however, a good town for jazz musicians. For the moment the city was, as the expression went, "wide open" – by both Canadian and US standards. Work was abundant: if opportunities to play jazz were generally restricted to after-hours jam sessions they were nevertheless plentiful in a city whose nightclubs might close only briefly before the lunch hour for a quick sweep of the floor and a fast wipe of the table tops.

Montreal's black jazz musicians were more of a community than its white musicians, although a community by default. Just as the *boulevard* St-Laurent has traditionally divided the French/east end from the English/west end in Montreal, Dorchester (now the *boulevard* René Lévesque) was an informal demarcation of black from white, to the point where a white musician who played for Charlie Parker would remember, mistakenly, that the black pianist Harold (Steep) Wade was probably not involved, adding by way of explanation, "Steep was part of the below-Dorchester crowd." Or, as another participant in the Parker episode put it, Wade and the city's other black musicians "were confined to the St-Antoine barracks."

Montreal "below Dorchester" was a world apart, one that the passing years have invested with a certain romance. Novelist Morley Callaghan set his novel *The Loved and the Lost* (1951) in part at the "Café St-Antoine" – in reality, the Café St-Michel – at Mountain and St-Antoine.

The Corner, as the intersection was familiarly known, was a quick, dark walk down Mountain Street from Dorchester, under the railway overpass that established the right side of the tracks from the wrong. The Corner's reputation was known far and wide: American musicians visiting Montreal invariably headed for Mountain and St-Antoine after their own concerts at the Forum, the Seville or Her Majesty's Theatre were over.

One itinerant American, trumpeter Louis Metcalf, led the International Band at the Café St-Michel from 1947 to 1950. (Under different names Metcalf and some of his musicians appeared in *The Loved and the Lost*, two of them serving Callaghan as secondary characters.) The International Band has been credited by historian John Gilmore in *Swinging in Paradise* with introducing bebop to Montreal, although members of Al Cowans' Tramp Band, among them tenorman B.T. Lundy and trumpeter Buddy Jordan, had arrived from New York by 1948, bringing with them first-hand knowledge of the revolution underway in Harlem and along 52nd Street.

Louis Metcalf was not himself a bopper, but rather an older-fashioned, Armstrong-styled trumpeter who had worked with the likes of Sidney Bechet, Duke Ellington and King Oliver; the Montreal musicians at his side nevertheless gradually mastered the new music with his blessing, if not his direct involvement.

Steep Wade was the quickest study. Other bop-inclined members of the International Band included the French-Canadian violinist Willy Girard, the Japanese-Canadian trombonist Jiro (Butch) Watanabe and the Swedish-Canadian drummer Mark (Wilkie) Wilkinson. Despite the demands of the shows they were hired to play, the young Montreal musicians managed to work in enough bebop during the intermission sets to satisfy themselves.

White Montrealers with vicarious tastes frequented the St-Michel, upstairs at 770 Mountain, as well as Rockhead's Paradise almost directly across the street at 1258 St-Antoine. Any less fleeting interaction between the city's white and black population was not, however, regarded with great sympathy in the early 1950s, save on the bandstand and perhaps at the ballpark – it was with the Mon-

treal Royals in 1946 that Jackie Robinson had broken the color bar-
rier in professional baseball en route to joining the Brooklyn Dodgers.
Indeed, Callaghan's *The Loved and the Lost* draws much of its drama from the tension created in the black community by a young
white woman's friendship with the "Café St-Antoine" musicians.

The International Band, hailed in 1947 as "a challenge to racial
prejudice" by the Montreal *Standard*, typified the loose mix of the
St-Antoine musicians. Most, but not all, were black. Some, like
Steep Wade, were Montreal-born. Others, like Metcalf, were
Americans who ventured up from New York and stayed for shorter
or longer periods. A young Sonny Rollins, for one, is remembered
by local musicians to have spent several months in Montreal, ca.
1950. It has also been suggested that Charlie Parker may have spent
some time in the city during the same period.

Uptown – "above Dorchester" as it were – there was no focus
comparable to The Corner. Of course, white musicians had the run
of the entire west or east ends of Montreal, according to their mother tongue, although the work available to both English and French
in dance orchestras, show bands and lounge groups offered even less
opportunity to play a little jazz.

Few Montreal jazzmen, black or white, would have thought of
their music as an art form. By profession, they were simply employ-
ees of the city's burgeoning entertainment industry; by preference,
they played a music that was of foreign origin. Jazz in Montreal, no
less than anywhere else in Canada, lagged far behind the other arts
in terms of self awareness, let alone self sufficiency – far behind
Paul-Émile Borduas and the group of Montreal painters known as
the Automatistes, for example, who had issued their passionate
manifesto *Refus global* in 1948.

In 1952, however, one young, white Montreal musician, Paul
Bley, not yet 20, saw the potential in a united front. And so the Jazz
Workshop was born. It lasted scarcely a year, an idea still well
ahead of its time. In the following decades, Montreal would have
several similar, musician-run operations, but not for another 25
years, when the Ensemble de musique improvisée de Montréal was
established in 1978, would it have one of any permanence.

Paul (Buzzy) Bley and Keith White made each other's acquaintance in 1949 – so the latter remembers – at Lindsay's, a furniture emporium of several floors on Ste-Catherine near Peel. Pianists frequented the store in search of an instrument on which to practise, while jazz fans haunted the listening booths in Lindsay's record department, checking out the latest releases. Both the pianists and the jazz fans begged the indulgence of the sales personnel; White subsequently married a salesgirl from the record department.

Bley and White met in the record department and then adjourned to one of the showrooms to demonstrate their respective accomplishments at the piano. White was limited to boogie-woogie, but Bley, who that same year succeeded Oscar Peterson at the Alberta Lounge, was already conversant with bebop.

"I was awestruck," White writes in his unpublished autobiography, *Noting the Scene*, "for here was this fellow, a bit younger than I and he was already talking the language."

Buzzy Bley, so named for a front-heavy haircut that put his friends in mind of a cartoon character of the day, left Montreal for New York in 1950 to study at the Juilliard School of Music, and for the next three years commuted frequently between the two cities. "When I left town," he said years later, "it was a *perfect* opportunity to put (the nickname) to rest."

Back home for the summer of 1952, he contacted several local musicians, White among them, with a plan to establish a jazz workshop, an organization that would be funded out of the musicians' own pockets for the purpose of establishing an all-hours venue for rehearsals and jam sessions.

The idea, Bley recalls, was based on drama workshops of the day – "to have an informal get-together of people rehearsing on the stage, so to speak." The emphasis was not on "performance-level performance," but on "the impact of first meeting..."

According to White's manuscript, dues were set at $25. Contributing members included the two founders, as well as a third pianist, Valdo Williams, the saxophonists Bob Roby and George Kennedy, bassists Hal Gaylor and Neil Michaud, the vibraphonist/pianist Yvan Landry and drummers Floyd Williams and Billy Graham.

To add to the workshop's financial solvency, Saturday afternoon concerts with Montreal musicians were organized at one of the city's premier nightclubs, the Chez Paree. Promotional and organizational assistance was provided by the Emanon Jazz Society, an organization of local jazz enthusiasts headed up by John Lymburner and yet another young pianist, Alfie Wade, Jr.

The concerts, remembers Lymburner, "would promote both the idea of the Jazz Workshop, which was taking shape, and the aims of the Emanon Jazz Society, which were to get more jazz into the city."

The first concert (August 23, 1952) netted about $300 (at $1.25 per ticket), the second (September 13) brought in about $250, and the third (October 4), $100. At one point, White records, the Workshop's bank account held nearly $1000.

After the second concert, the workshop signed a two-month lease for a third-floor room over the Video Café on the south side of Dorchester near Crescent; the lease was subsequently renewed in November for a six-month period and the space was used for Workshop and Emanon meetings and, beginning in February of 1953, for evening performances.

Meanwhile, the workshop's fourth concert at the Chez Paree, October 25, featured its first out-of-town guest, the New York guitarist Chuck Wayne, lately a member of the George Shearing Quintet.

Of course Bley, by then back at Juilliard and increasingly active on the New York club scene, was strategically placed to find musicians for the workshop's concerts. "I seem to recall bringing up people I had a working acquaintance with, as opposed to calling on the phone and saying, 'My name is... Would you please come to Montreal?'"

After a hiatus of several months, the workshop planned its fifth concert for February 7, 1953. It proved a prelude to the most intense period of the workshop's short history.

This time, the out-of-town guest would be Charlie Parker.

Paul Bley had jammed in New York with Charlie Parker at sessions organized by the saxophonist Joe Maini.

In the course of subsequent events, Bley would come to be reminded by Bird of his own father. "He had the same kind of voice as my dad, a deep voice, and he was a smaller, shorter man, sort of rotund, which my father was. I was charmed by him."

Parker in fact stood almost five-eleven; his weight fluctuated with his health. Bley stands a few inches over six feet.

As the pianist had learned from their meeting at the Maini sessions, Bird was sharing a basement in Manhattan's East 70s with several other musicians and working only sporadically, taking jobs of one or two nights' duration – Mondays at the Bandbox, for example, and the occasional trip to Washington. His reputation as an unreliable booking was now irreversible.

By his own account of the events, Bley thus assumed that Parker would be willing to make the trip to Montreal. *Pre*sumed, in fact.

"I knew about it," the pianist remembers. "That didn't mean that *he* knew about it."

Indeed as Bley tells it, telescoping the time frame, Parker found out only when the tall, self-confident young Canadian turned up at the door of his basement quarters.

"I knew the story," Bley noted in 1984, referring to Parker's reputation. "I'd been filled in about everything. I knocked on the door, and invited him to the Workshop.

"He said, 'When is it?'

"I said, 'Now – we leave in 20 minutes.' There was no use in discussing anything in advance with him."

Bird apparently agreed immediately, just as Bley had expected. "He was totally out of work, totally without funds. And the money was right."

Not only would Parker play at the Chez Paree on Saturday, but Bley had arranged an appearance the preceding Thursday on a local TV show, co-incidentally called "Jazz Workshop," thereby doubling the saxophonist's take from the trip into the range of a few hundred dollars.

"The question," explains Bley, "was not whether he would accept the gig, but whether he would show up for it."

If Bley was reminded by Parker of his own father, he himself speaks rather paternalistically of the saxophonist. At that, his suggestion that he accompanied Parker from New York to Montreal and back – that he "took [Parker] by the hand," as he put it to Len Lyons in

1977 – must be questioned. On the day of Parker's flight, the pianist – so other Jazz Workshop members suggest – was already back in Montreal.

However late Bley left his invitation, the Montreal jazz community knew by Wednesday, the 4th, of Parker's imminent arrival. Columnist Pat Pearce of the *Herald*, the only local newspaper to acknowledge the saxophonist's expected visit, ran a short item that read in part, "Charlie 'Bird' Parker, most popular alto saxophonist playing in the modern-jazz idiom, will be guest star at a Jazz Workshop of Montreal jazz concert at the Chez Paree Saturday at 2 p.m."

No mention was made, however, of Parker's guest appearance, Thursday at 8:30 p.m., on CBFT's "Jazz Workshop." In any event, Pearce would have had to know of Parker's visit no later than the 3rd.

Ironically, more notice was taken by the media that week of the advent of a jazz policy under the Jazz Workshop's sponsorship at the St. Moritz Roof on Ste-Catherine near Mansfield. Both the *Herald* and the *Gazette* ran items in their show-biz columns.

According to the latter, "The Montreal counterpart of New York's jazz haven, Birdland, is set to open this weekend at the revived St. Moritz, atop the Maroon Club. Tenorist Brew Moore, Dick Garcia, guitar, Phil Arabin [sic], drums, and Montrealers Neil Michaud, bass, and Buzzy Bley, piano, will comprise the first group."

Again, no mention was made of the same musicians' appearance Thursday on "Jazz Workshop." However, ads placed on the 4th in both papers filled in the details of the St. Moritz engagement: the club was to open on Friday the 6th, hours would be 9 p.m. to 2 a.m., and admission was set at 98 cents.

Thus, there would be four New York jazz musicians in Montreal for the weekend...

Charlie Parker...

Brew Moore, 28, so named for his preferred beverage; he had played tenor saxophone in the Claude Thornhill Orchestra, with the Gerry Mulligan and Kai Winding groups and in less formal circumstances around New York alongside Charlie Parker...

Dick (or Richie) Garcia, who at 21 had already recorded with George Shearing and worked casually in New York with Parker, including a Sunday afternoon session two weeks earlier at the Hartnett Music Studios, where Bird was approached by four members of the Toronto's New Jazz Society with plans for a concert in May...

Phil Arabia, mis-identified by the *Gazette* but described in the *Herald* as being "ex- [Terry] Gibbs."

Even at four, the New York contingent was strong enough, together with a supporting cast of Montreal musicians, that Bley would come to view the three days of unprecedented activity – the TV show, the inauguration of the Jazz Workshop's policy at the St. Moritz Roof and the concert at the Chez Paree – as the city's first jazz festival, distant predecessor to the celebrated Festival International de Jazz de Montréal of the 1980s.

Bob Roby was at his home on Lajeunesse in the north end of the city on Thursday afternoon. He was waiting for the phone to ring. Then 27, one of the Jazz Workshop's older members, the alto saxophonist had been hired on a standby basis for "Jazz Workshop" to play in the event that Charlie Parker failed to arrive in Montreal as scheduled.

He was, he believes, recommended by Paul Bley, with whom he had previously played in and around Montreal. Roby was basically a "club dating" musician, as he puts it. With Bley, however, he played jazz.

"In fact, we worked the whole summer at a lodge up north at Ste-Agathe. Billy Graham was on drums. It was only a trio. No bass. And we almost only played jazz. Can you imagine? We didn't have to play shows, so it was a lot of fun – a whole summer of revelations."

To play a jazz gig *in* Montreal in 1953, then, was a rare enough opportunity, let alone to do so on TV in Charlie Parker's stead.

Naturally, Bird was one of his idols. Roby had met Parker briefly in a Boston club the year before.

"I went to talk to him after a set. For some reason or other, I was very nervous, I didn't know what to say about the music, so I said to Bird, 'I hope God keeps you with us for a long time.'

"His eyes got big, he looked at me, and he said, 'Thank you.'"

On the afternoon of February 5, Roby was again very nervous. "Then we heard that Bird was at the airport. I really felt a lot of relief."

When Parker landed at Dorval, he was greeted by the familiar figure of Neil Michaud, at 20 the youngest of the Jazz Workshop musicians. The two men had met at least once before, when Michaud accompanied Bob Roby to Boston. The bassist was delegated by the Jazz Workshop to await Parker's flight, get him to a connection if necessary and then deliver him as quickly as possible to the CBC studio in the old Ford Hotel on Dorchester.

During the ride downtown, Michaud unexpectedly found himself listening to Parker hold forth on a recent New York City Ballet presentation of Stravinsky's *The Firebird* at the New York City Center. Parker's interest in Stravinsky has been well documented, but what had obviously captured his imagination in the NYCB's production, remembers Michaud, was George Balanchine's choreography.

Bird was in town. So too, by some other route, were Brew Moore and Richie Garcia, together with drummer Ted Paskert, another Claude Thornhill alumnus and, apparently, a last-minute replacement for Phil Arabia. "At the time," Paul Bley explains, of his insistence on having a New York drummer, *any* New York drummer, "it seemed like a great effort for someone to keep time in Canada on drums." Little more is known of Paskert than of Arabia, save one Montreal fan's memory that he was indeed "a rock-steady drummer" and thereby met Bley's requirements.

To play for Charlie Parker was, inevitably, to wait for Charlie Parker. Bird was late for the TV show. In his absence, the others rehearsed, perhaps took a quick meal at the bus station nearby or somewhere up on Ste-Catherine and traded the latest news and gossip.

The *Metronome* readers' poll had just been published in the February issue; Pat Pearce of the *Herald* had made reference the previous day to Parker's recent first-place showing among altoists in both the *Down Beat* and *Metronome* polls. No surprise there: Parker had won the *Metronome* poll regularly since 1948. And no surprise, either, that Montreal son Oscar Peterson, just three years into an international career, would top the piano category for the first time. Of more immediate interest, though, Dick Garcia had placed 12th among jazz guitarists, and a few Montreal musicians had turned up in the results; two, in fact, were present for a time at the TV studio and would play for Parker at the Chez Paree – Billy Graham, who placed 14th among drummers with 16 votes, and Hal Gaylor, who tied with Red Callender for 16th among bassists, receiving 11 votes.

And there was news from the world of boxing that so interested jazz musicians of the era. A return bout had been announced on the 4th between Jersey Joe Walcott and Rocky Marciano. In a memorable fight the previous September in Philadelphia, Marciano had taken the heavyweight crown from Walcott in the 13th round. The rematch was set for Chicago Stadium, April 10.

CBFT, Channel 2, went on the air in September of 1952. "Jazz Workshop" began on December 11. The half-hour program was described in a Montreal *Devoir* TV listing for December 18: "Jazz recital by the best artists of the metropole. Guest singer." By the sixth telecast, February 5, neither black musicians nor Americans were new to the show. Pianist Valdo Williams and bassist Bob Rudd had already appeared, as had pianist Perry Carmen's quartet, trumpeter Allen Wellman's sextet, pianist Roland Lavallée and the visiting Delta Rhythm Boys.

Pierre Mercure, a contemporary classical composer, was the show's producer, advised by Don Cameron, a former dance-band drummer who had made his career as a DJ and CBC radio actor. Cameron in fact served as emcee of both "Jazz Workshop" and the Saturday afternoon Jazz Workshop concerts at the Chez Paree, which no doubt facilitated Parker's appearance on the TV show.

Early television productions were "a little loose-ended," according to Cameron, who had a large studio clock placed at the foot of one of the cameras as a point of reference to keep the show more or less on time. Telecasts went live-to-air before a studio audience, and naturally the possibility – followed soon enough by the fact – of Parker's delayed arrival was cause for concern. "That was part of the tension, part of the nerves, the frustration. If somebody, or something, didn't show for rehearsal, that would help tighten the screws, because we were live."

Parker and Michaud made it to the studio in time, however, arriving to find the audience abuzz. With television so new, Michaud explains, "everyone was excited because there were going to be [on-camera] shots of the audience. It was a very hyped-up atmosphere. The musicians were tuning up, the noise was very loud – nobody was paying much attention."

Parker unpacked and assembled the Grafton alto. Its white body blazed under the studio lights. Fitting a reed to the mouthpiece, he played a couple of runs. The studio, Michaud recalls, fell silent immediately. "His sound was so big – I'd never heard anybody play that loud before. All he did was play a couple of scales, but it cut through everything – drums, piano, the lot..."

Once on air, "Jazz Workshop" proceeded smoothly through at least eight tunes. The program had been rehearsed by Bley and the other musicians, but "when Bird went on," Michaud remembers, "he just called over his shoulder 'Cool Blues in C.' He called every tune from that point on. I think we ended about half a second out from where we started. And the producers were ecstatic; first of all they were freaking that he was just calling everything from the front, and then of course in the end they were delighted because it had run so perfectly."

A tape of "Jazz Workshop," made on a machine apparently patched into the speaker wires of Keith White's TV set, catches the wisk of brushes at a medium-fast tempo. After four bars, a bass enters, followed after four more by a piano. The pattern is repeated before the trio moves into Lester Young's *Jumpin' with Symphony Sid*, the theme song of New York DJ Symphony Sid Torin, whose broadcasts could be picked up in Montreal, 530 km away. The musical allusion would surely have been lost on most "Jazz Workshop" viewers, although the Emanon gang in the studio audience were no doubt nodding knowingly as the trio repeated the catchy 10-note riff over two, 12-bar choruses.

Don Cameron: [in a Tony Randall kind of voice] *Good evening ladies and gentlemen. Tired of the everyday songs on the hit parade? Wanna get away from it all? We offer you the Jazz Workshop! Once again CBC TV has pleasure in inviting you to join us at these week-*

*ly get-togethers, where tonight we'll be offering you variations and
musical interpretations by various American and Canadian musicians. Several weeks have passed since our last program and, also,
my spies tell me that a number of people have been buying new television sets, so it could be some of you people watching our show
tonight are seeing it for the first time and are beginning to wonder
what it's all about.*

The program, Cameron continues, is "a sort of haven for jazz
musicians where they can get together and compare musical ideas –
sort of compare notes – and play the kind of music they like."

The Paul Bley Trio, with Michaud and Paskert, is formally introduced in George Gershwin's *'sWonderful*, given a spirited, extended
performance that finds the pianist moving perhaps a bit stiffly but
without hesitation between the pure bop that he was hearing in
New York and the more generic, and slightly more dated swing-
based style common to his fellow Montreal pianists of the late 1940s
and early 50s.

There follows, in turn, an unrevealing Cameron-Bley exchange –
the pianist announces the opening of "Montreal's own Birdland,
right here in Montreal, tomorrow night" – and the introduction of
"another lad," Dick Garcia. The quartet plays Garcia's *Johann
Sebastian Bop* in an appropriately contrapuntal fashion, leading to
the guitarist's hard, crisply-inflected solo, the first strict bebop of the
evening.

Don Cameron:...*Our outstanding jazz artist this evening on the
show, a man that we're very proud to be able to bring to you people
here in Canada, possibly the gentleman who's considered tops on
the alto saxophone, Mr. Charlie Parker...* [applause] *Charlie!...* [off-
mike] *It's all yours, boy...* [on mike] *Good to see you, Bird...*

Charlie Parker: [deep, formal voice] *Good to be here...*

Cameron: *Fine. Could this be your first trip to Canada?*

Parker: *In many a year, yes...*

Cameron: *Many a year. Well, how would you like to kick off
with something in a nice bouncy tempo to get us all warmed up?*

Parker: *All right. I think first I'll take a tune that was recorded on
the Dial label, 1948,* Cool Blues. [rolling 'Cool']

Cameron: [mimicking] Cool Blues. *Here it is.*

Unknown voice: *Let's go...*

Parker likely appeared to "Jazz Workshop" viewers much as he appeared to any other audience. There was a gentleness in his handling of the saxophone. His eyes were usually open as he played, his face impassive, his body steady, his hands motionless save for the occasional slight shift at the wrist, and his fingers moving almost imperceptibly with just the quick, occasional jump of his left index finger. Nothing in the mere *sight* of Parker in performance, save for a spreading sheen of perspiration, even hinted at the expression, the emotion or exertion of his solos.

His history on this occasion is a bit shaky – *Cool Blues* was first recorded in February of 1947 – but his solo is a solid, seven concise choruses of sustained intensity. Blues had long been his métier; the *Hootie Blues* that he recorded with Jay McShann 12 years before was a revelation to musicians who had heard neither of Bird nor of any saxophonist who played as Bird did.

Parker's original version of *Cool Blues* had brought him the French Grand Prix du Disque, and the tune itself, a bouncing, four-bar piece of melodic filigree thrice repeated, was a standard item in his club repertoire during the early 1950s. As played on 'Jazz Workshop,' *Cool Blues* is taken at a tempo markedly faster than that of the original, and Parker substitutes a slurred urgency for the Dial's dry articulation and lingering lyricism.

Two and a half minutes later, Bird had *arrived* in Montreal.

Don Cameron: [applause] *We are going to bring Mr. Charlie Parker back a little later, ladies and gentlemen, for another solo. We are quite sure you would like to see him again... In the meantime, though, we'd like to switch to the female side of our show this evening. We've gone a couple of programs without a girl. Tonight, we'd like to bring you a very charming personality in Miss Laura Berkley. Laura, can you make your way* [tape stops]

Berkley, so unceremoniously denied a small place in history, was appearing at the time in a revue at the Downbeat, where she was billed as "Montreal's latest singing sensation." Remembers Don Cameron, "She was certainly the type of gal you'd want to see on TV – she was young, pretty and she could sing."

Don Cameron: [applause] *Well, we'd like you to save some of*

*that applause, because the next gentleman – also all the way up
from New York City – plays a fine tenor sax, Mr. Brew Moore.
Brew, c'mon up here, take a bow. Just before Brew made his
appearance, I asked him what he'd like to play. He said, "It's called*
Bernie's Tune. *Maybe you'll recognize it. However, it goes something like this. Gentlemen?*

Following so closely after Laura Berkley, Brew Moore would
have presented "Jazz Workshop" viewers with a startling sight. His
hair slicked back from an alternately sunken and billowing face,
unshaven either way, he played saxophone out of the left corner of
his mouth and held the horn at a close angle to his body in emula-
tion of one of his two idols, Lester Young.

Moore's other idol was standing just offstage, and Moore could
not hide his nervousness in Parker's company. His feature on "Jazz
Workshop," *Bernie's Tune,* was a line written by Bernie Miller and
recorded a few months earlier by Moore's close friend Gerry
Mulligan. It was apparently one of Moore's favored tunes at the
time; he would play it again at the Chez Paree two days hence.

Despite his familiarity with the piece, he never quite gets a firm
grip on his solo. Lesterish in its tone and easy lope, and Parkerish in
some of its construction, it slips on him, its rhythmic balance turning precarious in a way that makes a straightforward statement
seem rather strained and just a little poignant. Garcia and Bley follow for 32 and 24 bars respectively, the pianist's confidence growing
with every solo.

Don Cameron: [applause] *The tenor saxophone artistry of Brew
Moore, ladies and gentlemen... We promised you another appearance by Charlie Parker. Come on up here, Charlie, with that horn of
yours.* [Dryly] *We seem to have got ourselves into the habit, Charlie,
of asking our artists to introduce their own selections. How 'bout it?
What are you going to do for your second one tonight?*

Parker: *Well, I think for our second one, we'll try another one of
the Dial label's, released about 40... '48 – 1948 that is. Let's try*
Don't Blame Me...

Voice in audience: [swooning] *ohhh...*

Cameron: *It's all yours, boy...*

Parker: [with child's innocent lilt] *Okay...*

Don't Blame Me, in fact recorded late in 1947, is the program's only ballad. Over a solemn tempo, Parker's mercurial solo captures a succession of moods and attitudes – wistful and hurt through Jimmy McHugh's melody, and then coy, mischievous, taunting and once again suitably abashed in the space of the chorus that follows. The piece becomes a study in character, a three-minute autobiography that seems to echo the ambivalence that Parker demonstrated throughout his life about responsibility.

Don Cameron: [applause] *What say, ah, what say we keep Charlie Parker onstage, bring back for a final ensemble selection, Mr. Brew Moore on tenor sax? Brew?*

Brew Moore: [off-mike] *Uh-huh.*

Cameron: *Grab your horn, c'mon up here.*

Moore: [off-mike, something like] *That's great, yes.*

Cameron: *I think, now that we have everyone assembled, we might kick loose with a tune that seems to be a favorite among jazz musicians, a little ditty called* Perdido. *Here it is.*

In fact, Parker, Moore and Garcia play Benny Harris' rarely-recorded *Wahoo*, a descending, terraced line based on the chord changes of Juan Tizol's *Perdido* and titled in honor of Harris' Indian ancestry. Parker divides the bridge into two cheerful phrases and sustains the lighthearted mood throughout the first solo, bearing down and drawing back almost imperceptibly in a gentle play of tension. His closing run, a spinning, vaguely modal line fashioned in triplets, makes a further allusion to Indian origins of both the tune's title and its composer, drawing a loud guffaw from someone in the band.

Moore in turn sounds more confident with Parker right at his side. He repeats a bouncing, four-note figure from Parker's penultimate phrase, and fashions it into a short, deferential solo, rather plainer in design but direct and not without a certain drive of its own. After a chorus of fours between Bley (two), Paskert (four) and Garcia (two), Parker's audible instruction, "Bridge!" introduces a second, bursting eight-bar alto break again taken in two fanciful phrases, and leads to a single reprise of the theme.

Don Cameron: [applause] *Well, to the gentle strains of* Perdido, *we must unfortunately bring this particular program to a close.* [Bley, Garcia, Michaud and Paskert begin to play softly at a medium tempo.] *I think we created a small piece of musical history tonight here in Montreal, with featured work by Brew Moore, Charlie Parker, Buzzy Bley, Neil Michaud, let me see, Dick Garcia and Ted Paskert on drums...*

Next week we'll be offering you a contrast in music. We have the music from the Deep South, from New Orleans, styled by Russ Meredith and his dixieland sextet...

The telecast over, the six musicians stepped down from the low stage and the audience rose from its wooden chairs. Some of the bolder fans approached Parker, among them a boyish, bespectacled teenager.

Still a few weeks shy of 18, Len Dobbin was a familiar figure in Montreal jazz circles. He had often requested records on local radio – in later years he himself would become the English voice of jazz in Montreal, as well as a columnist for *Coda* and the *Gazette* – and his name was already known to the Emanon Jazz Society recruiters who burst in on him one day, at some point in 1951, while he was checking out new releases at Lindsay's. "They were astounded," he remembers, "that I was this little kid."

After the show, Dobbin was delegated to inform Parker and Brew Moore of the evening's social agenda. "People were getting Bird's autograph, so I waited in line. Being the great humorist that I am, once I got closer I asked if anyone had a blank cheque. Bird thought that was incredibly funny and cracked up.

"I told him that there was a jam session at the Latin Quarter.

"He said, 'Fine.' So we all headed over to the Latin Quarter – never to see Bird."

Nor to see Brew, who apparently went instead to visit a friend, the fan dancer Sally Rand, whose New York revue was in town at the Beaver Café that week.

Moore may have had other concerns as well. At some point soon after the telecast, he learned that the Jazz Workshop's arrangement with the St. Moritz Roof had, for reasons now forgotten, fallen through. However, the band was quickly moved to the Jazz Workshop's third-floor room over the Video Café.

Fans arriving on Friday night were directed to the café, two blocks down and a half dozen blocks west. The *Herald*, clearly the most supportive of Montreal's newspapers, ran a photo of a pensive Brew Moore on the following Tuesday, although the cut line would have had jazz fans still looking for the quintet at the St. Moritz Roof.

Bird loved Westerns. There were two opening in Montreal on Friday, his day off, *The Mississippi Gambler* with Tyrone Power at the Strand and *Montana Belle* with Jane Powell at the Princess Theatre.

The Stars and Stripes Forever, with Clifton Webb as John Philip Sousa, was new at Loew's, as was *Eroica, The Beethoven Story* at the Avon, *Les Miserables* at the Capitol and *Kansas City Confidential* at the Orpheum, all perhaps holding a certain perverse interest for Parker.

Bird also loved to take hansom cabs through Central Park. Montreal, of course, had its *calèche* rides up Mount Royal.

Precisely *what* Parker did on Friday is not known.

He was, however, expected that night – Brew Moore's first – at the Jazz Workshop's room over the Video Café. Keith White was waiting with a tape recorder. Parker was on his way sometime before midnight, or so White heard later, when he fell into a conversation with a couple of fans outside his rooming house a couple of blocks away.

Huguette Rajotte, a small, slim woman in her early 20s, rode a Vespa motor-scooter and haunted the expresso bars that turned Stanley Street around Ste-Catherine into a short stretch of bohemia after dark. Rajotte was the secretary of the Emanon Jazz Society.

On Friday night, in the company of another Emanon member, Willie Lauzon, she went down to The Corner in search of information. By 11 p.m. they had found out what they wanted to know: Charlie Parker was staying that night in a room up on Stanley Street.

"So I said to Willie, 'Let's go ring the doorbell!' Of course, Willie is behind me – he doesn't want to do anything. But I said, 'Listen, this is fantastic: Charlie Parker is in town. We *have* to meet him.'"

They found the address, rang the doorbell and asked to see Parker.

"The first thing I knew, Charlie Parker is down – his room was on the second floor. He's down and at the front door.

"He said, 'C'mon in,' and invited us upstairs."

There were twin beds in the room and little else. Parker sat on one, Rajotte and Lauzon on the other.

"We talked with him for about two hours. I guess at that time he was pretty much in bad shape. He was perspiring a lot. What he was saying, his speech – everything – was all right, but he was really perspiring, which was not necessarily very normal...

"At the time, we knew what he was doing, who he was playing with, where he was playing, the problems he was having – although we didn't talk about *them*... It was really all music. I don't think we even talked about Montreal. It could have happened in a room in Chicago, or Paris, or London, and it would have been the same. We had a great musician there, and there was only one subject. There was no other subject..."

Around 2 a.m., Charlie Parker lay back and promptly fell asleep.

"Willie looks at me and says, 'Listen, we're not going to stay here all night and watch the guy sleep.'

"I said, '*Yes!* This is Charlie Parker sleeping!'"

Lauzon left. Rajotte remained.

"It was kind of... not scary, but very weird, because he was sleeping, and during his sleep, he whistled. He was whistling *April in Paris*... I just watched, amazed."

Parker awoke about 10 a.m. Rajotte, who had been too excited to sleep more than fitfully on the other bed, accompanied him to breakfast in a Stanley Street restaurant. Parker ordered bacon, eggs and toast. Rajotte had coffee.

"I remember the service was slow, and I thought to myself, 'My God, don't they know who he is?' But then, how would they? Who knew who Charlie Parker was in Montreal? Nobody, except people like Len [Dobbin], myself, Buzzy Bley and the local musicians."

Parker was clearly impressed with his young companion.

To Hugette [sic], he wrote on a scrap of paper imprinted with a sketch of a driver in his *calèche*, overlooking the city from atop Mount Royal...

It's always pleasant
to meet Good people
Such as yourself.
wishing you the best
of everything
Charlie Parker

Showtime at the Chez Paree, a half block below Ste-Catherine on Stanley Street, was 2 p.m.

Huguette Rajotte had parted company with Parker late in the morning. "There was a sort of distance between a fan and a star and I sensed, 'I can't hang onto this guy.' I'd received so much, just talking for hours with him, that I was sort of overwhelmed. It was out of the question that, between 11 and whenever the concert was, I should even be around."

Instead, she met up early with Willie Lauzon and other members of the Emanon society, determined to get a good table stageside at the Chez Paree. The club, built on a square plan, held a total of about 300 at the street level and up in a balcony that wrapped closely around the thrust of the room's stage. A plain drape curtained off the backstage area at the proscenium. Painted figures loomed on the back wall directly above. To the left, two smiling entertainers – Fred and Ginger types. To the right, the prophetic image of a nude woman, hi-ball in hand, reclining against the thumb of an oversized, white-gloved hand. By 1960 the Chez Paree would be a strip club; for the moment, though, it specialized in the premier touring acts of the day, not the least of them Frank Sinatra.

The afternoon began with a quintet that would later record under the Discovery label as the Canadian All Stars – altoist Al Baculis, pianist/vibraphonist Yvan Landry, pianist/accordionist Gordie Fleming, bassist Hal Gaylor and drummer Billy Graham. There were also sets by a Paul Bley trio and by Brew Moore, probably with Bley, Dick Garcia, Hal Gaylor and Ted Paskert.

Backstage, Bert Joss of Soundscription Service, a small recording company and retail hi-fi outlet in Montreal, had – at Keith White's behest – patched a Webcor tape recorder into the Chez Paree sound system.

Nearby, heated discussions were underway among various Montreal musicians as to who of their number would accompany Parker. Keith White writes in *Noting the Scene*, "Jazz Workshop members were adamant in their view that they should have first choice in the matter since this was all financed by the Jazz Workshop. After that one was settled, they started to argue violently about which member was going to play with Bird. One decision had unanimous approval. Paul Bley was not going to play with Bird at the concert because he had already played with Bird on the TV program."

By the same logic, it was Hal Gaylor, then 25 and just three years away from taking his career stateside, who would play bass for Parker at the Chez Paree. Neil Michaud, meanwhile, had other duties on this afternoon.

As vociferously as some workshop members asserted their right to play with Parker, others quite willingly deferred.

White himself was one. "I wasn't too interested because I didn't think I was competent enough."

Yvan Landry was another. "They asked me, 'Would you like to play with Parker? I said 'Yes.' And then I said 'No, I don't think so.' I was afraid, you know."

Billy Graham, 24, was a logical participant, both as a Jazz Workshop member and as one of the city's best bop drummers in the three years since his arrival from Winnipeg. He remembers the opportunity in a different light. "I never gave it a thought that I shouldn't [play]. You get sort of mesmerised, you follow directions, you're there and of course you're going to do it. I couldn't have cared if I'd fallen on my face. I would have done it, just to be there. I don't know what kind of attitude that means I had at the time, but... if there's a meal in front of you, you might as well partake of it."

As the Montreal musicians argued for a once-in-a-lifetime chance to play with Bird, Parker himself had other, more routine concerns.

"Bird wouldn't play unless he got straight," remembers Emanon's Alfie Wade Jr., who had been working behind the scenes on the concert. Early in the afternoon, Wade and Neil Michaud took Parker by cab to the St-Antoine district where Steep Wade – no relation – lived in a rooming house known as The Orgen. Steep Wade was also a heroin addict; similarly, he drank heavily. He would die under mysterious, though certainly intoxicant-related circumstances before 1953 was out.

The connection was made openly and without ceremony. Parker, Wade recalls, "was kind of aloof. He was cool. He didn't say a whole lot. I don't remember any really super-friendly conversations. He was pretty business-business." He was also, remembers Michaud, in no great hurry to go anywhere in particular afterward. "We had a hell of a time getting him to the concert."

Parker, the two Wades and Michaud finally arrived at the Chez Paree well after 4 p.m. Brew Moore was onstage. The entire concert had to finish soon after 5 p.m. in order that the club could be readied for Frank Sinatra's performance that night. Parker would have had just time enough to observe Bert Joss monitoring the Webcor recorder backstage – it was obviously running as Moore wound up his set with *Bernie's Tune* – and to borrow a necktie from a bystander. Nevertheless, the Joss tapes of the concert reveal no great urgency as Don Cameron takes the stage around 4:30 p.m. to introduce the afternoon's special guest.

Don Cameron: *Let me see now, we'd like to bring back, ah, Hal Gaylor and Dick Garcia on bass and guitar respectively. Gentlemen, are you out there? Hal? And Dick?* [Applause] *Good. And let's bring back the fellow who helped us open the show. On drums, Mr. Billy Graham. Billy!* [Applause, shouts of "Yeah, Yeah."] *At last report, our pianist was Steep Wade. Steep, are you there?* [Applause, off-mike voices: 'No! Valdo!'] *Oh, now it's been changed to Valdo Williams, well...* [Huge cheer] *Every day something new... Well, we have gathered, ah, what we consider, ah, as good a combination of musicians as we possibly can in order to background a gentleman, I suppose, that most of us consider way-up, number-one, top man on alto sax, CHARLIE PARKER!* [Cheers, applause, whistles.]

Charlie Parker: [off-mike] *Thank you, thank you.*

Cameron: *Ladies and gentlemen...*

Charlie Parker with Hal Gaylor (partially hidden), bass, and Billy Graham, drums. Photograph by Huguette (Rajotte) Schwartz.

Parker: [inaudible]

Cameron: [laughs] *Man, they've been waiting! We asked Bird about what he'd like to say. He said, Man, I just don't talk, I wanna play* How High the Moon. [A cheer.] *So here it is.*

Valdo Williams, it seems, had jumped the gun, which was fine with his fans, out at the Emanon table, who sent up the cheer that signaled his arrival onstage. Williams, a New York musician who spent the early 1950s in Montreal, was a local favorite.

"Valdo," remembers Billy Graham, "got so excited at the announcements, man, he ran up on the stage. So *he* was the one who started. To me – I mean, I love Valdo, but his 'time' was not Steep's 'time.' Steep and I had been doing a lot of playing together, so it was very easy just to do the right thing. But Valdo was really excited – the first tune, he started off an introduction and it got a little faster and it got a little faster, and the bass player and I, we just couldn't come in!"

Indeed, the opening eight bars of *Ornithology*, Parker's theme based on *How High the Moon* and first recorded for Dial in 1946, are a three-man race to the starting line.

"Bird's standing there," Graham continues, remembering his vantage point to the left onstage, a few feet behind Parker. "He was very calm, and he was turned sort of sideways, halfway to the audience, watching the band. He finally realized, like, nobody could find *it*. You *could* have, but we *all* had to find it together. So he just turned around and started. Everybody just *went* to him. We didn't stand a chance. As soon as he started we were in business. Just like that. Like magic. It wasn't like he was loud, or that he gave a downbeat, he just started, from a standing position..."

Yvan Landry was watching from the Chez Paree balcony, having declined the opportunity to join Parker onstage. "I remember he started to play, he turned around, and he looked at the pianist. I said, 'Oh, oh, there's something wrong, there's something not going the way he likes.'"

Once Parker establishes the theme of *Ornithology*, the band falls into place. Graham's cymbal ride is steady and quick and in the manner of a Max Roach. Williams, however, never quite settles down. Parker is more reckless than he had been two nights before; the bite, the light growl and the bright squeal in his first chorus seems to give voice to the excitement in the room. He faces no restrictions this time. If, finally, there would be perhaps only 10 or 15 minutes more available to him at the Chez Paree, in view of his late arrival, then the additional time comes without the need to accommodate the sort of formalities that he had faced on the TV show. This is Parker's set alone, although Williams and Dick Garcia would each have the opportunity to solo at length.

Garcia, in fact, followed Parker on *Ornithology*. Bird drifted backstage. There he found Bert Joss again running the Webcor. Remembers Joss, Parker "proceeded to expostulate loudly that he had an exclusive recording contract with Mercury Records and we weren't permitted to record him. We assured him that this was just cheap home equipment and it would certainly not be a professional quality recording and couldn't be used for records. Little did we know..."

Of course, as the only musician "on mike," Parker would come through loud and clear on any recording made directly off the club's sound system. Moreover, Parker's solos would realistically be the only point of interest to jazz history. "Quite frankly," comments Paul Bley, "it wasn't the first time that he had people in the background who were mercifully *under*-recorded..."

In response to Parker's complaints, Joss made a show of turning off the tape recorder during Garcia's solo and put down the machine's lid, fully concealing the reels. As Parker returned to the front of the stage, Joss started the Webcor again, leaving the lid closed.

The recording of the concert was interrupted at least once in this manner and, according to Keith White, possibly more often. Indeed there are various discontinuous breaks on the surviving tape of every tune that Parker played, save the ballad *Embraceable You* in which, significantly, he was the only soloist. Invariably, either the Garcia or Williams improvisation is affected by the interruption; Parker, naturally, would not have been paying attention to Joss during his own solos. Ironically, in view of Parker's apparent consternation, virtually everything that he played at the Chez Paree is intact.

Parker's second Montreal version of *Cool Blues* is taken at a medium-up tempo; the urgency heard in his solo on the TV show is replaced by something quite unhurried, even playful, as he takes some alternate melodic routes through the changes, moving out in the passing lane, as it were, or driving up the shoulder, but never at a loss for speed or control. Most of Garcia's solo is lost, although an extended and somewhat heavy-handed Williams improvisation solo remains. Bird trades fours with Garcia before dovetailing neatly on the fly with the tune's theme.

Parker called an intermission.* Both Huguette Rajotte and Keith White made their way backstage, Rajotte with a request for the se-

---

*See Discography, p. 102-103fn

cond set and White to handle the saxophonist's objections to Joss' activities. Parker, obviously intrigued by unusual musical instruments, had momentarily put the Grafton alto aside and was toying with Hal Gaylor's five-string, Wilfer bass. The other musicians hung back, according to White, unwilling to make an approach.

White introduced himself as co-director of the Jazz Workshop. Parker, he recalls, clearly was not happy. "He looked like he was ready to wrestle some bears or something."

Mustering up his courage, White made his pitch. "I sort of explained that I wanted the recordings for posterity, for the Workshop's records. And he bought that, which was true at the time."

As White remembers it, Parker's mood changed quickly. "He looked me up and down, as I was giving him my best spiel, and then he grabbed my hand and pumped it. Oh, he was very friendly. He got me off balance, because I was ready to start arguing. He was very charming... 'Well, I am very pleased to meet you. You want to make some recordings? Why certainly... Just sign a paper saying you'll never release them without my permission.'

"I had a little notebook in my pocket. I whipped that out, wrote something, signed it, and handed it to him. He said, 'Fine,' and pumped my hand again. 'Very nice to have met you. You can record anything you want.'"

Unlike the other Montreal musicians onstage at the Chez Paree that afternoon, Bob Rudd and Harold (Steep) Wade were older than Charlie Parker, the bassist by a month and the pianist by about two years.

Rudd was born in Toronto but raised in Nebraska and had worked in the 1940s on the US West Coast with Noble Sissle, Sid Catlett, Lucky Thompson and Gerald Wilson before settling in Montreal toward the end of the decade. He may well have known Parker from their respective sojourns in Los Angeles.

Wade, on the other hand, was born near The Corner in Montreal and had rarely strayed far from home. He worked in Ontario briefly as an alto saxophonist with Mynie Sutton's Canadian Ambassadors, ca. 1939, and as a pianist with trumpeter Jimmy Jones in 1943, but the exigencies of his heroin addiction — the same exigencies

Parker was facing in Montreal – made travel difficult.

Wade had been *the* jazz pianist around Montreal prior to the emergence of Oscar Peterson in mid-decade; by the time the younger man made his move onto the US circuit in 1950, Wade was a fading force. He left Louis Metcalf's International Band that year and for the next three – in fact the last three of his life – he was in poor health, worked only intermittently and stayed close to the Orgen rooming house. Nevertheless, his reputation was established locally, and visiting musicians carried his name stateside.

Emanon member Carlton Baird, who first heard Wade at the Café St-Michel, remembers him as one "one of the best 'compers' I've ever heard. I don't know what the man's secret was, because Steep wasn't that young, but when the bebop movement came to Montreal, he was right there with it, from note *one*."

Wade's early experience as a saxophonist was significant; he most certainly would have been familiar with the kind of singularly linear thinking that characterized the new music.

As drummer Wilkie Wilkinson, who heard Wade on a nightly basis from the other side of the footlights, suggests, "Anybody that blew a horn was more than delighted to get hold of Steep."

Both Baird and Wilkinson agree: Wade comped like Bud Powell. For Parker, of course, that would have been ideal.

The tapes were rolling again. If Parker had been placated during the break, the Joss tape of the afternoon's three remaining tunes still shows evidence of further interruption. No spoken introduction survives of his accompanists for the second set, but Dick Garcia had returned, Steep Wade was now at the piano and Bob Rudd took over on bass. The drummer was Bobby Malloy, 22, a highly-skilled showband musician who would soon leave Montreal with teen idol Paul Anka and eventually settle in Las Vegas.

The Joss tape picks up the performance towards the conclusion of the head on *Moose the Mooche*. Parker's choice of the tune at the very least holds a certain irony in view of Steep Wade's assistance earlier in the afternoon, and the identity of the immortalized Moose The Mooche, one Emry Byrd, who had kept Parker supplied with heroin during a trip to California in 1945.

Wade's firm hand at the piano is immediately apparent; his chords have tremendous harmonic bite and judicious rhythmic placement. Malloy, meanwhile, is game but overmatched. Where Bill Graham had provided efficient backing and otherwise laid low, Malloy is more combative, putting a heavy foot to the bass drum and squaring off his accents in a way that succeeded only in threatening the balance of Parker's solo. Bird, of course, is not thrown off, even through a series of awkward fours with Malloy and Garcia that precedes a return to the theme.

Parker approached the microphone. No longer acting the honored guest, as he had on TV, he is now the genial entertainer, talking at a higher pitch and at an excited, uneven tempo. His repeated, off-mike "Thank you" is clipped to a single word that rises in pitch – "Youp... youp..."

Parker: *Thank you, thank you, ladies and gentlemen. And for the next tune, we'd like to care for a request from some very dear friends of mine... here in Montreal... We'd like to... give our rendition of...* Embraceable You. *We sincerely hope you'll enjoy it...*

Bird's second ballad performance in Montreal is again mercurial, if ultimately less evasive than *Don't Blame Me*. Like most of the other tunes he played during the visit, it comes from his most productive period of recording, for Dial in 1946 and 47.

After Wade's spare, three-bar introduction, Parker plays the Gershwin theme lightly and affectionately, with just a hint of exaggeration. His solo is a fickle creation, no more than a series of fanciful, if virtuosic embellishments on the original melody, lingering over one phrase and racing through the next. Instead of a final reprise of the theme he fashions a familiar cadence on *In an English Country Garden* leading to a long, trilled note that swells before he cuts it off abruptly.

Parker: [quickly, then slowing] *Thank you, thank you very much, ladies and gentlemen... Thank you very much... At this time, we'd like to keep the show underwhy* [corrects himself] *underway by playing a tune, an oldie. Uh, this was done for the Savoy label. On the Savoy label it was released, I think, about 1945. It was amongst the first that was done on the Savoy, down in New York. We sincerely hope that those of you who haven't heard the tune before will still... like...* Now's the Time...

The final tune of Parker's visit was a blues that dated back to his first recording session under his own name in November of 1945. Countless versions later, the composer sounds a little flatfooted on the "Hucklebuck" figure of the head, but is in full flight by the second bar of his first chorus, running long flurries of 16th notes that are broken only by the occasional turn of 32nd notes. He seems to relax at the sound of Garcia's entry on the third chorus, and his remaining choruses are full of squealing, laughing, teasing, cajoling, swaggering and rollicking lines.

The Joss recording cuts Garcia off after the guitarist's first chorus and resumes with the final notes of Wade's solo; the moment in the Chez Paree session that surely would have held the greatest historical significance, Parker's confrontation with the city's premier bopper – moreover a musician who survives on just one 78 and a few amateur recordings – has been lost.

Don Cameron: *Thank you Charlie*

Parker: [to audience] *Thank you...* [to Cameron] *Pleasure to be here.*

Cameron: *Anytime... Fine... I guess that's it, ladies and gentlemen... Sorry!... We would like to mention once again, you can catch the imports from the States* [tape stops]

While the principals of the Jazz Workshop were congratulating themselves, another group of younger Montreal musicians were making an approach to Parker. Vic Vogel was one of their number. The leader of Montreal's most important big band through the 1980s was 17 years old in February of 1953 and already playing piano in the city's east-end clubs.

More than once he made the trip across town – across Ste-Catherine, by the cross streets with good French names like St-Dominique and Jeanne-Mance, along past Lindsay's – to hear the Americans presented by the Jazz Workshop at the Chez Paree and upstairs at the Video Café.

Vogel was not always impressed. "It was supposed to be some sort of dialogue, but I found the local guys were doing most of the talking. It was not an earth-shaking experience. Usually the wrong

people were asked to play all the time. The right people were either
too humble, or they were from the east end. There was still that
thing at the time..."

Then as now, the east end of Montreal was a mosaic of ethnic
communities. Vogel, for example, was of Hungarian ancestry. The
trumpeters Guido Basso and Walter Battagello came from Italian
families. Many more musicians were, of course, French.

"We all went to the west end later – '59, '60 – when there was a
need for larger groups, which they had plenty of in the east end.
Little by little, some guys would come to the east end and listen, and
play, and *hear* what was going on. The west end guys were very
English... even in their style of playing. They were still listening to
Harry James when we were listening to Dizzy Gillespie. They were
still trying to get the damn vibrato like Harry James – to get the
schmaltz going. We were trying to get *rid* of the vibrato.

"When we got to the west end, everybody'd say, 'How come you
have no vibrato?'

"We'd say, 'What's a vibrato?'"

Accompanied by some east-end musicians on this early trip to the
west end – they probably walked the dozen and a half blocks, since
no one had a car – Vogel sought Parker out at the Chez Paree. He
was not, and never would be, intimidated by visiting Americans. "I
remember him as being pleasant. I didn't know what to expect,
maybe, but there was nothing harsh about the man."

Naturally, the group tried to entice Parker back to their home
ground. "We asked him to come to the Domino – to play at the
Domino, because [pianist] Bob Langlois was there.

"He said, 'Ah, I'll get there, I'll get there.'"

Notwithstanding Paul Bley's claim in 1984 that he "took [Parker]
back to the plane... and delivered him safe and sound to that funky
basement where I found him," few of the Workshop or Emanon
members have any memory of either the events immediately following the concert or the details of Parker's return to New York. Bley in
fact would have been working with Brew Moore upstairs at the
Video Café.

Parker was seen at some point Saturday evening at the Latin

Quarter, where there was again a jam session. Bob Rudd played, right ear pressed as always to the neck of his bass, but the identity of the other musicians – a guitarist and a trumpeter among them – is not known.

For a time, Parker listened from the bar. Pressed at one point for a comment on one of the soloists, he is remembered by Bill Graham to have offered the diplomatic response, "He has a lot of technique." Later, Parker sat in.

Indeed he seems to have been on his best behaviour throughout his three days in Montreal, playing remarkably well and deporting himself most congenially. "I never saw a man who was more in control of his faculties and of what was going on," Graham recalls. "Everyone else was in a dither except him, both at the CBC and the concert. Literally. He was like a magnet. He made me nervous in that other people were nervous *because* of him. Once I realized it was them, and not me, it was OK."

Of course, even without the element of uncertainty that surrounded any Parker engagement by 1953, the mere prospect of playing with Bird would have been enough to intimidate many of the Montreal musicians. "I don't think anyone was up to it," Graham suggests, "except maybe Steep. Well, that's not entirely true – everybody was *capable* of it, but not used to the idea."

Paul Bley, who would surely have been the least intimidated, is more severe in his assessment. "Everybody didn't know how badly they played until that performance. He defined the centre of the aesthetic and left all of us wanting." Graham's recollection of *Ornithology*, from the ninth bar on, puts the experience in more immediate terms. "It was like riding a fire engine around a corner at 90 miles an hour – you're just hanging on by the tips of your fingers."

Massey Hall

Had Charlie Parker nothing else to look forward to as he made his way back to New York from Montreal – there would in fact be a broadcast with the Bill Harris/Chubby Jackson Herd from the Bandbox on the 16th, and a performance with The Orchestra in Washington on the 22nd – he nevertheless held a contract with the New Jazz Society (NJS) of Toronto for an appearance at Massey Hall on May 15.

The contract, dated January 26, 1953 (though probably signed the previous day), has been reproduced in *To Bird with Love*. The job would last from 8:30 to 11 p.m. Parker would be paid "$200 [plus] 21.7% of the musicians' share of the net profit." The $200 was "to be paid before the commencement of the engagement; the percentage to be paid immediately after the engagement." Signed by Dick Wattam of the NJS, the contract was "cancellable to May 1, 1953, without mutual obligation."

Unlike Parker's Montreal performances, though, and indeed unlike much of his itinerant work during this period, the saxophonist would appear with four other musicians who could reasonably be numbered among his few peers in modern jazz. Now in the company of the irrepressible Dizzy Gillespie, a distracted Bud Powell, the volatile Charles Mingus and a controlled Max Roach, Parker was a rather less vivid presence, no longer *the* man of the hour.

There were times when he dropped from sight altogether.

Bird, remembers one witness to the events at Massey Hall, "said nary a word and blew like crazy."

There were no clear lines drawn on the basis of color or language on the Toronto jazz scene in the early 1950s. The story here was much simpler, indeed much shorter. If the Toronto scene was in most respects behind Montreal, though, it was also in one respect different: to some degree it had already institutionalized jazz. Before jazz musicians could break completely free of the city's dance bands, the best of their number went into city's studios. In neither case was jazz the exclusive, or even primary, focus of their activities.

Were there any lines at all on the Toronto scene of the early 1950s, they might simply have been drawn between those jazz musicians who worked for the CBC and those who did not. The distinction would hold for the better part of the next 25 years. Eventually the CBC gigs – the jazz shows among the more common "variety" work – took their place with all the other studio assignments that were available once the city became the centre of the English-Canadian entertainment industry with the advent in 1952 of television.

There were CBC radio jazz shows through the 1940s and into the 1950s, in particular "1010 Swing Club" and its successor as of 1948, "Jazz Unlimited" – record/concert programs whose very names reflected the shift of local interests, as well as local musicians, from swing to bebop. Each show featured Toronto bands in concert at the CBC's Grenville Street studio and, from time to time, at Massey Hall. Bandleaders included the clarinetists Bert Niosi and Cliff McKay from the old guard and trumpeter Graham Topping and tenorman Roy Smith from the bop generation. Musicians were generally drawn from a pool of the younger players; when Topping and Smith were not out front, they would take a place in their respective sections.

And there was, new for 1953, CBLT's "Jazz by Jackson," featuring the Philadelphia pianist Cal Jackson who, by virtue of his frequent appearances on "Jazz Unlimited" and his residency at the Park Plaza Hotel, was a relative celebrity among the city's jazzmen. Although the Saturday-night series made its debut January 10, a full month after "Jazz Workshop" was seen in Montreal, it was nevertheless described by Toronto *Telegram* columnist Helen McNamara as the "first jazz show to be produced on Canadian TV," perhaps an indication of just how little attention the jazz communities in the country's two largest cities paid to each other.

The Park Plaza, on Bloor Street at Avenue Road, was one of just two Toronto nightspots to feature jazz musicians on a nightly basis. The other, the Colonial Tavern (on Yonge Street just below Shuter and around the corner from Massey Hall) presented U.S. stars. Ethel Waters, George Shearing, Earl Hines, Mel Tormé and Stan Getz performed there in the early months of 1953; the Lionel Hampton Orchestra was in town for the week of May 11.

Lounges with liquor licenses were in fact relatively new to the city and still, in 1953, uncommon. No judicial commissions into vice and corruption would be necessary in Toronto The Good; the hotbed of nightclubs in which jazz had flourished in Montreal since the 1920s had no parallel in Toronto. The Silver Rail, a few doors north of the Colonial at the corner of Yonge at Shuter, was Toronto's first licensed lounge, opening as recently as in 1947. It would have a small place in the story of Jazz at Massey Hall, but no particular significance in the story of jazz in Toronto.

Outside of the CBC, Toronto's modernists in early 1953 played in semi-privacy at the House of Hambourg, a coffee house run by Clem and Ruth Hambourg midtown on Bloor Street, and at the Jazz Artists Club, which intermittently set up shop at a Lithuanian hall in the west end of the city. The city's traditionalists were heard at the Maison Doré on Asquith Avenue near Yonge and Bloor, a mere hurled epithet from the House of Hambourg.

Beyond the CBC, jazz fans listened to Joe Rico from Buffalo and to WABC from New York. The latter, at 770 on the AM dial, could be pulled in after the CBC station CBL, at 740, left the air; among WABC's late-night shows were regular broadcasts from the club named in Charlie Parker's honor, Birdland. In 1953, Parker was still a regular performer there.

Thus bebop in its purest form was heard locally on a somewhat distant or impersonal basis – via radio or on record, the latter purchased from the Promenade Records (on Bloor at Bay) or Premier Radio (on Yonge, below College), which served Toronto much as

Lindsay's served Montreal.

The "live" event of any year was still the swing-oriented Jazz at the Philharmonic, usually held in late September or early October at Massey Hall. Bop's innovators and most influential figures were infrequent visitors to the city; its more temperate popularizers, the Shearings and the Getzs, enjoyed a presence at the Colonial, for example, that its pioneers did not.

Indeed, the fact that a seminal figure like the pianist Lennie Tristano would have appeared in at the United Jewish People's Order Hall on Christie Street in July of 1952 was due only to the efforts of the recently-formed New Jazz Society.

Buoyed by the concert's success – some 400 people attended, according to a review in *The Globe and Mail*, and the Tristano quintet's performance was deemed worthy of release on record as *Live in Toronto 1952* (Jazz Records JR-5) some 30 years later – the NJS began to lay plans for a second event that would again address the absence from Toronto stages of some of bop's other major figures.

Members of the NJS met at each others' homes to listen to music and at the House of Hambourg or the nearby Diana Sweets restaurant to discuss business.

On one such occasion, NJS member Art Granatstein remembers, "We were just chatting and somebody said, 'Hey, who would *you* like... what do you think of *this*?'

"The names all just seemed to pop out.

"'Wouldn't *that* be *some*thing.'

"It was just a matter of pulling the names out, writing them down, and saying, 'This would be the greatest thing in the world!'"

But which names? Charlie Parker's, certainly, and those of trumpeter Dizzy Gillespie and drummer Max Roach, all participants in bebop's first recording sessions from 1944 and 45. A couple of bassists were considered, Oscar Pettiford and Charles Mingus, while the NJS' initial choice of pianist, according to the society's president and the concert's driving force, Dick Wattam, was Lennie Tristano.

Wattam, a parts clerk at General Electric, was in his early thirties, a little older than most of the NJS members. "He was always so enthusiastic, and you got caught up in his enthusiasm," remembers one, Gary Dutton. "He tried to run the society as a sort of little fief," remembers another, Boyd Raeburn*.

Several NJS members were Tristano fans or acolytes, Wattam foremost among them, so the choice would have been natural. Tristano in turn apparently suggested Bud Powell as a more logical pianist for the occasion. Powell, however, would be in Creedmore, a New York mental hospital, until early February of the following year.

It was also Wattam's intention that Sarah Vaughan would sing at the concert. Vaughan, after all, had appeared on record with Gillespie and Parker – and they in turn with her – as early as May of 1945. Another NJS member, Jack Batten (later jazz critic for *The Globe and Mail*), remembers suggesting trombonist J.J. Johnson when budgeting for the concert seemed to allow for a sixth instrumentalist. The idea was quickly dismissed by Wattam, who scoffed, "Of *course* not, he works in the post office anyway."

Wattam had other grand schemes as well. Dancers from the Royal Winnipeg Ballet would interpret the music of the New York musicians. The National Film Board would document the performance. The CBC would record it. The event would be billed as the First Annual Festival of Creative Jazz with the implication that there would be others. A Toronto big band would open the concert.

"It's true," Wattam comments in retrospect, "that some of us were obsessed with putting this thing on, and others were not as enthusiastic." Among the latter, the NJS's secretary-treasurer, who – remembers Wattam – resigned "because she was sure [the concert] was going to be a financial disaster and didn't want to have anything to do with it."

Boyd Raeburn: "Dick was a bit of a dreamer. He couldn't equate the costs of the concert with the capacity. You'd say, 'Dick, [even] if you sell all the seats, it won't cover all the expenses you're proposing.'"

Gary Dutton: "Everybody said, 'Fine, but what about the money?' That never worried Dick. It was 'Damn the torpedoes, straight ahead.'"

In the end, the Ballet, the Film Board and the CBC all declined to

---

* Not the popular dance band leader.

participate. The grandiose billing stood and a Toronto big band was indeed added to the program, although in truth a musicians' union regulation required that local musicians be hired, if not necessarily used, whenever visiting musicians performed within its jurisdiction. Faced with the expense, the NJS chose to put the local's members to work.

By mid-January of 1953, the concert had been set for Friday, May 15, a date with no more significance than the fact that it was the birthday of Wattam's daughter. Massey Hall, with seating for 2765, had been booked. At least some of the proposed musicians had been contacted by telephone.

On Friday, January 23, 1953, four NJS members, ranging in age from late teens to early thirties, piled into a car after work – or, as

Art Granatstein at the Hartnett Music Studios, NYC, with Charlie Parker. The identity of the drummer is unknown. Photograph courtesy of Arthur Granatstein.

the case of at least one of their number, after school – and drove all night to New York City.

Dick Wattam remembers the trip as "really great; the weather was really rather spring-like for a day – there was a thaw." The others – Art Granatstein, Bill Hoare and Roger Feather, the last a student at Lawrence Park Collegiate and "somewhat precocious when it came to jazz" – variously remember a snowstorm, fog, slippery roads and lost bearings. It was, in Hoare's words, "a desperate drive down."

Taking turns at the wheel, the four arrived around breakfast time on Saturday morning and checked into the Taft Hotel. After a short rest, they set out to find the musicians.

Parker signed a contract dated January 26 – the following Monday, by which time the Canadians, tired but excited, were safely back in Toronto – on a piano bench at the Hartnett Music Studios in the Warner Theatre Building on Broadway near 48th Street. Parker was playing an informal session – "one of the greatest performances of Parker that I've ever heard," recalls Wattam. "The performance at Massey Hall was a very exciting performance; the performance at Hartnett's was very laid-back and relaxed... I was so knocked out by the music, I could hardly type the contract."

Granatstein's recollection of Parker, some 10 days before the saxophonist's trip to Montreal, corroborates Paul Bley's description of a musician down on his luck. Parker arrived at the Hartnett studios with only a mouthpiece.

"Poor Bird," Granatstein recalls, "looking so lost and sheepish at this session. All he had was the damn mouthpiece. Someone had to pinch an alto for him... I surmised, because of his general air and the demeanor of various other people, that he was somewhat impecunious and he simply didn't have a horn. Either he had hocked it, lost it, or something had happened, and he simply didn't have one."

Of the musicians contacted during the trip, Parker is remembered as the most openly enthusiastic about the Massey Hall concert. "Bird was really the pussycat of them all," according to Granatstein. "He was really desirous of getting together [with the others], and expressed it by signing up as readily he did. He was a sweet guy, and he really went for it, really liked the whole bag."

In view of the miscellaneous jobs and sidemen that were more and more Parker's lot by 1953, the prospect of playing again with the likes of Gillespie, Roach and the others in a major – and familiar – concert hall would surely have been attractive. Indeed Parker may have even regarded the reunion as a first step toward turning around a flagging career.

Gillespie, meanwhile, was reached at his apartment, and Roach was visited in Brooklyn. Mingus was also contacted, according to Granatstein, although the bassist apparently did not immediately agree to participate; his name would not be among those initially announced for the concert. This, contrary to accounts (including his own) that he was in fact responsible for organizing the quintet.*

At the time of the Canadians' visit, in fact, Mingus was at least a temporary member of the Duke Ellington orchestra and, in view of the esteem in which he held Ellington's music, very likely was hoping to extend the job for as long as possible. His celebrated run-in with Juan Tizol, the bassist bearing a fire axe and Tizol a bolo knife, brought the affiliation to a sudden conclusion on February 3, leaving Mingus to "start with the gigs again," as he put it in his autobiography, *Beneath the Underdog*.

Bud Powell, meanwhile, remained in Creedmore until the 4th and would ultimately be signed through the Moe Gale Agency.

Unlike Parker, Gillespie and Roach apparently were somewhat guarded when presented with the NJS offer. The response came as something of a surprise to the Canadians. "You know," comments Granatstein, "we, being members of a club, thought that this would all be a little more chummy."

The trumpeter was "rather brusque and very businesslike, which made me feel a bit uncomfortable, because I was a neophtye when it came to this sort of thing." Roach in turn was "very charming, but again somebody who was thinking about everything. He wasn't emotional, not 'Oh yeah, *great*, guys, yeah!' Which is the way

---

*Mingus told Mike Hennessey (*Down Beat*, 13 May 1971), "The Massey Hall gig was mine – a guy wrote from Toronto asking me to bring a band up so I got the musicians together." Bill Coss, in his liner notes to the release of the quintet's performances under Mingus' Debut label, wrote, "Running into early trouble, the [NJS] finally contracted with bassist Charlie Mingus to bring... a group to Canada."

Parker was, more or less."

Naturally, there were requests for guarantees of various sorts – conditions for which the Canadians weren't quite prepared. "I think what happened was, we said, 'Yeah, yeah, we'll look after it, we have the money in Toronto.' We did *not* actually have the money in Toronto. We went to [the loan company] Household Finance. That's partially how we got the money."

The musicians were signed to individual performance contracts. On paper at least, the band had no leader. There were, Dick Wattam explained years later, egos to consider. "We felt at our end that we might have some trouble if we designated one musician as leader, because of their personalities. Here were five musicians at the pinnacle of their abilities and fame at the time. Well, is Charlie Parker to be the leader? Or Dizzy?"

The NJS' egalitarian approach did not, however, extend to the fees paid to the musicians. Parker would receive $200 plus the promise of a percentage of the unspecified "musicians' share" of the profits. Gillespie negotiated for $450, while Roach signed for just $150.

Bird was in Montreal when news of the First Annual Festival of Creative Jazz was announced in Toronto. Alex Barris devoted the entirety of his *Globe and Mail* column, "The Record Album," on February 6 to the event, noting that Dizzy Gillespie, Charlie Parker and Max Roach were "definitely set" and would be "augmented by a pianist whose name we are not at liberty to mention yet."

The pianist in question was probably Bud Powell, who had been released from Creedmore just two days earlier. The lack of any reference whatsoever to a bass player suggests that the identity of the fifth musician still very much up in the air.

In addition, Barris wrote, "there will be Calvin Jackson leading a 17-piece band drawn from the ranks of the best available men in Toronto. That means, no doubt, that the band will be substantially the same as that used on the weekly Saturday night TV show, Jazz With [sic] Jackson, and also on the monthly live Jazz Unlimited sessions."

Barris continued, prophetically, "Whatever the NJS intention may be, it seems a fair bet that the local men and the guests will top off the evening by joining forces, or at least forming impromptu groups to add some unscheduled spice to the concert."

The festival, Barris warned, would be "sold on a subscription basis because the cost of bringing together such an assortment of musicians is not inconsiderable and can be met (if you will keep in mind the lack of any NJS treasury) only if a minimum of 1,500 tickets are sold before May 1."

The *Telegram*'s Helen McNamara noted the concert in passing in her column "McNamara's Bandwagon" of February 7 ("We've just had word that..."). *Down Beat* magazine's Toronto correspondent, Robert Fulford, quickly sent off an item which appeared in the March 11 issue and again underlined the necessity of selling 1500 tickets ("about 1/2 the house") by May 1.

In the following issue of *Down Beat*, March 25, Fulford wrote (possibly filing as late as the third week of February), "The New Jazz Society still had no pianist or bassist to work behind Dizzy Gillespie and Charlie Parker... but was negotiating with several."

Some accounts of the concert raise the possibility that Oscar Pettiford was also under consideration as the bass player for the quintet. Indeed, as an early 52nd Street associate of Parker, Roach and Gillespie, he might have seemed a more logical choice than Charles Mingus, a West Coast musician who, at 30, had made New York his base just two years earlier. Pettiford would certainly have been a logical alternative in view of Mingus' committments to Duke Ellington at the time. Moreover, Pettiford was playing with Bud Powell in the weeks immediately following the pianist's release from Creedmore, precisely the period in which the NJS was attempting to complete the quintet.

Confusing the issue is Max Roach's assertion (in Gillespie's autobiography *To Be or Not to Bop*) that Mingus was a "substitute bassist for Oscar Pettiford who had broken his arm playing baseball, or something like that, with Woody Herman's band." The baseball game in question, however, took place in July of 1949; Pettiford was playing again by 1950.

Mingus offered a different scenario in a Toronto radio interview, May 17, 1975, with CJRT-FM broadcaster Ted O'Reilly. "To tell you the truth, I didn't want to make it. Dick Wattam insisted I make it. I told him, 'You should get Oscar Pettiford.'"

Pressed to explain his lack of interest, Mingus said, "Because I wasn't a bebopper, man. I was never a fan of bebop. I was a Duke Ellington fan. If you notice, none of the beboppers have ever been fans of Duke's. Charlie Parker never recorded *one* tune of Duke Ellington's. And bebop is an inferior music to Duke; it's far inferior to the harmonic complications that Duke has worked out in music."

As for Pettiford's lack of interest, it is known that he and Gillespie had a falling out as early as 1944. The bassist's career took a different turn and the two men did not record together again. Pettiford, remembered (in Ira Gitler's *Jazz Masters of the Forties*) as a proud, volatile man who was jealous of Gillespie's fame, may simply have had his own reasons for declining any offer to participate to a reunion.

The matter was resolved soon enough. "McNamara's Bandwagon," in the *Telegram* of March 14, announced the addition of both Mingus and Bud Powell to the quintet, noting that they had been "just signed up this week."

The pianist, benefitting from representation by the Moe Gale Agency, would receive $500, the highest fee paid to any of the five musicians. Mingus, like Max Roach, agreed to $150, bringing to $1450 the total fee for the quintet.

There are also conflicting accounts regarding the decision to record the concert. Specifically: who made it, to whom that decision was conveyed, and when? Both Dick Wattam, on behalf of the NJS, and Max Roach, co-partner with Charles Mingus in Debut Records, claim the original idea as their own.

It had been Wattam's intention to have the CBC record the event. The facilities were in place: concerts by the Toronto Symphony Orchestra were broadcast from Massey Hall, as was the occasional big band performance heard on "1010 Swing Club" and "Jazz Unlimited." However the CBC, according to Wattam, declined the opportunity in the absence of the appropriate recording contracts between the NJS and the New York musicians.

At the same time, Debut Records was moving into its second

year. By May of 1953, the company had recorded two somewhat
unusual Mingus quintets – each had a cellist and a singer – and a
vocal quartet known as the Gordons. But the Debut catalogue had
nothing with either the musical or commercial potential of the five
musicians scheduled to play in Toronto. The decision to record the
Massey Hall concert was, according to Roach, "just natural for us."

In any event, there was communication – indeed, co-operation –
between the two parties on the project. According to Wattam, prof-
its from the recording would be split six ways between the NJS and
the musicians, although no contract was ever signed to that or any
other effect. It was agreed that Mingus would obtain a new, high-
quality Scotch recording tape just introduced in the USA but apparently not available in Canada. In turn, the NJS would supply an
Ampex tape recorder secured for the occasion by Wattam from
General Electric. The Ampex was also ahead of its time in Canada;
a frequency converter was required to boost Massey Hall's power
source from 25 to 60 cycles in order to run the machine.

There may not, however, have been any discussion among the
five musicians about the recording. Mingus and Roach, of course,
knew of the plan. The three others very likely did not.

The concert was now two months away. With everything in place,
the NJS could only sit back and wait as each its members took an
allottment of tickets to sell to friends and other fans. The society
would, however, face a few unexpected developments in the coming
weeks.

Further investigation proved Calvin Jackson's orchestral jazz
inappropriate to the evening. A substitute was found: the so-called
CBC All-Stars, in fact a rehearsal band led for the occasion by trumpeter Graham Topping and drawn from the pool of musicians who
regularly played on the CBC's "Jazz Unlimited." Topping was first
mentioned in this regard by Alex Barris in *The Globe and Mail* of
March 27.

Of greater concern, the much-anticipated rematch in Chicago of
Rocky Marciano and Jersey Joe Walcott, announced February 4 and
scheduled for April 10, was postponed to May 15 – the very night of
the concert. Moreover, the fight would be shown on home TV

throughout the U.S. and Canada, presenting a significant threat to the concert's drawing power in Toronto.

The NJS principals met to discuss the situation. They still had the May 1 escape clause in their contracts with the musicians but decided against exercising the option. "We were afraid," explains Art Granatstein, "that we'd never get these guys together again, especially with Bud's frail health and all the other circumstances of getting them to Toronto... We felt that we better go ahead regardless, and we took our best shot at it."

In late April, perhaps a small break: a double bill of Louis Armstrong and Benny Goodman scheduled for May 4 at Massey Hall was cancelled after Goodman collapsed of fatigue; the concert might have otherwise provided the Festival of Creative Jazz with still more box-office competition, at least for those few fans whose tastes spanned the growing number of styles in jazz.

With or without the competition, and however strong the NJS's resolve, the event was clearly in trouble. Reported Alex Barris in "The Record Album" of May 1: "The New Jazz Society has decided after a great deal of soulsearching to go ahead with its May 15 Massey Hall concert, despite the fact that advance sale is considerably below the safe mark."

Graham Topping, then 25, is remembered as one of the more gifted and most colorful musicians on the Toronto scene of the early 1950s and equally as one of its tragic figures in later years. He was, in the words of one of the musicians in his band at Massey Hall, "one of a kind. He was a character; he liked to live it up, used to drink a little..."

Some years after the Massey Hall concert, he was in a single-car accident that left him with a crushed hip; he continued to drink heavily and, following what a newspaper obituary euphemistically described as "a lengthy illness," died in 1976 at the age of 48.

Topping began playing professionally in his late teens and was soon heard frequently as a leader, arranger/composer and soloist on "1010 Swing Club." An original Topping composition from 1947, *Bop Goes McDougall*, presumably written for the show's host, Dick McDougall, dates the trumpeter's early interest – early by Canadian standards – in bebop. Dizzy Gillespie was the model for his playing and, by 1953, Woody Herman's bop-oriented big band had influenced his writing. Topping had become particularly adept at lifting Herman arrangements from records and from broadcasts that his friend, the tenorman Hart Wheeler, would tape off the radio.

By reputation then, Topping was a logical choice to replace Cal Jackson. As of May 1st, though, he was still scrambling to line up musicians for the CBC All-Stars. Six names were mentioned in "McNamara's Bandwagon" on April 25; another five were added in the same column on May 9. With the Massey Hall concert set for a Friday night, and payment at about $25 a man, Topping found himself in competition with local dance band leaders, Mart Kenney and Stan Patton in particular, for the services of the rehearsal band's regulars. The result – in the words of baritone saxophonist Norman Symonds, one of no less than eight subs – was "a mixture of odds and sods."

Alex Barris and Helen McNamara continued to plug the concert in their respective *Globe and Mail* and *Telegram* record columns. In a brief preview on May 9, McNamara quoted an enthusiastic Graham Topping, just returned from a California holiday, as saying, "There is as much going on here as there is in LA."

Meanwhile, Toronto's third major newspaper, the *Daily Star*, seemed to take no notice. On the day of the concert – and the Marciano/Walcott fight – it chose to run a photograph of the challenger's daughter playing piano.

NJS members appeared on various local radio shows to talk up the event. After one such spot, a CKFH announcer was pressed into service as the emcee for the evening*, filling in at the 11th hour for Dick McDougall who, according to Dick Wattam, had withdrawn his services in light of rumors out of New York that Charlie Parker had gone missing and would not be making the trip to Toronto.

It is known that Parker had played Birdland on Saturday the 9th, six days before the Massey Hall date. A recording of the WABC broad-

---

* Although he is remembered clearly by those involved with the concert, the announcer himself has no recollection of his participation in the event. He had, and has, no connection with jazz and shall remain nameless here.

cast with pianist John Lewis, bassist Curly Russell and drummer Kenny Clarke has been released under a succession of labels. It is also likely that Parker was estranged from his common-law wife, Chan, during this period. A telegram sent to Chan Parker at her mother's address on May 18, three days *after* the Massey Hall concert, suggests a separation, and also reveals something of Bird's state of mind: "...I WANT YOU TO KNOW THAT I AM IN THE GROUND NOW I WOULD SHOOT MYSELF FOR YOU IF I HAD A GUN BUT I DONT HAVE ONE... THE MOST HORRIBLE THING IN THE WORLD IS SILENCE AND AM EXPERIENCING SAME. I AM TIRED AND GOING TO SLEEP"

Came the day of the concert, the musicians gathered at LaGuardia Airport in New York. Powell was in the company of his legal guardian, Oscar Goodstein, then manager of Birdland. Mingus was travelling with his wife Celia. The others arrived alone. Some accounts have Parker missing from the party. The truth of the situation may lie somewhere in, or between, the various surviving scenarios, overlapping and occasionally contradictory as they are.

"We received a communication from Parker," Dick Wattam said in a CIUT-FM interview, May 9, 1988, "that he didn't want to fly. He did not like flying. Would we be good enough to send him train tickets instead of air tickets?... He got back to us a few days before the concert and said, 'I've got to have an advance, I'm short of money and I have to have an advance.' We found out later that he had tried to cash the rail fare but he hadn't been able..."

Parker, Wattam said, asked for and was sent $200.*

"And that was the last communication we had with him prior to the concert."

Wattam picked up the story in a later 1988 interview. "Dizzy came up to my apartment. My address, of course, was at the bottom of the contract. He announced that Bird did *not* take the train, that Bird and Dizzy both missed the flight to Toronto because Dizzy was looking for Bird in New York. Bird couldn't be found anywhere. I

---

* A variant, recounted by Wattam to Toronto *Star* columnist Peter Goddard in 1978, had Parker receiving his advance under the threat of accepting an offer to appear at The Casino in Toronto. However, jazz had come and gone at the Casino a few years earlier.

JAZZ FESTIVAL

DIZZY GILLESPIE — CHARLIE PARKER
BUD POWELL — MAX ROACH — CHARLES MINGUS
Plus CBC ALL-STARS • 17-PIECE ORCHESTRA
Led by
GRAHAM TOPPING
MASSEY HALL

TONIGHT AT 8.30 P.M.

Tickets Now at All Agencies and Premier Radio

Toronto *Telegram*, May 15, 1953.

believe actually Max found him somewhere. And they got him dried
out and I think either Max or Dizzy kept an eye on him for the next
few days. But they missed the main flight, which was Mingus, Max,
Bud Powell and Oscar Goodstein, and they had to take a later flight
to Buffalo."

A different account is offered in the original liner notes to the
Debut release of *Jazz at Massey Hall*. "Perhaps it's only of passing
interest," wrote Bill Coss, "but one sidelight of the trip is that, having arrived at LaGuardia airport, [the musicians] discovered that
only five of their party of seven, swelled by the presence of Mingus'
wife and Birdland's Oscar Goodstein, could take the pre-arranged
flight, [and] that two would have to wait for a later plane. By some
process of figuring they decided to leave [Parker] and Gillespie
behind, then spent many hours in Toronto wondering if they would
ever come."

Neither Dizzy Gillespie nor Max Roach, nor again Celia (Mingus)
Zaentz or Oscar Goodstein could confirm, deny or clarify any of
these accounts 36 years later. Of course what for the Toronto pro-
moters waiting at the Malton airport would be a once-in-a-lifetime
event was, for the New York musicians, simply another routine,
out-of-town, overnight trip.

Whatever the complications of the journey, Powell, Mingus, Roach and company arrived in Toronto first, followed in time by Gillespie with Parker. They all passed through customs, but not before the NJS was forced to post bond guaranteeing that they would not sell their instruments while in Canada. Once downtown, Powell, Roach, Mingus and, eventually, Gillespie headed for Massey Hall. Parker, meanwhile, almost immediately dropped from sight, prompting Gillespie to ask one NJS principal at the hall, "You *didn't* give him an advance did you?"

The Topping band was in rehearsal. Several of the Toronto musicians, including four of the five saxophonists, were reading most of the trumpeter's charts for the first time. The playing was labored. At one point, though, the music started to *move*. Surprised, the men in the horn section looked up and to their right. Max Roach had finished setting his drums in place – bass drum, snare, two toms, cowbell, hi-hat and ride cymbal, a modest kit by any standard – and had started to play along. "We were dragging or something," suggests trumpeter Erich Traugott, "and Max wanted to get us off our asses..." A couple of the Toronto musicians tried to return the favour later that afternoon by inviting Bud Powell out for dinner before the concert. The pianist was willing, remembers saxophonist Gordie Evans, but a mindful Oscar Goodstein thought better of the idea.

Bird's whereabouts remained both a mystery and a concern. He, at least, was on somewhat familiar ground in Toronto. Powell and Roach were probably making their first trips to the city. Mingus had played the Colonial Tavern as a member of the Red Norvo Trio in 1950, and Gillespie had been in Toronto as early as 1939.*

Some, if not all, of the musicians checked into the Ford Hotel, a relatively cheap, and certainly convenient establishment on Bay Street, across from the bus station. On this sunny afternoon, with

---

* Gillespie was once asked about other trumpet players who were investigating new chords in the late 1930s. He spoke of the Toronto musician Robert Farnon, then a member of CBC radio's Happy Gang and later a noted BBC arranger and composer, who "was playing cornet at this time, when I was with Cab Calloway. Cozy Cole, Choo [sic] Berry, Danny Barker, most of these guys would go over to this guy's house in 1939, way before he went overseas..." (*The Jazz Review*, January 1961).

the temperature in the low 60s, the Ford – one block north on Yonge Street and one west on Dundas – was a pleasant five-minute walk from Massey Hall. Other downtown hotels also figure in various accounts of the event, and it is quite possible that the musicians, individually contracted as they were, would have arranged their own accomodation prior to, or on, their arrival.

Indeed, it was at the Park Plaza that the NJS' Alan Scharf and Boyd Raeburn encountered Bud Powell. "We were standing in the entrance to the beverage room," remembers Scharf, "and Bud came up to us and said, 'Have you got any money?'

"This was just like in [the film] *Round Midnight*. So Boyd and I dug down in our pockets. Between us we had about 35 or 50 cents, and we gave this little bit of change to Bud, who immediately disappeared.

"We were still standing there, talking, when Mingus arrived from somewhere with his wife.

"He said, 'Was Bud here?'

"'Yes.'

"'Did you give him any money?'

"'Yes.'

"'How much did you give him exactly?'

"And then they went running off after Bud."

At 8:30, as specified on the contract, Charlie Parker turned up backstage at Massey Hall. He asked for Dick Wattam – Wattam had, of course, signed the contract. Parker offered no explanations. He made one request.

"When I met Bird at the stage door," he remembers, "he was in a beautiful mood, sober as a judge. Absolutely stone cold sober.

"He said, 'Dick, one thing... before I go on I have to have a drink.'

"I said, 'Fine, there's a bar right across the street, the Silver Rail.'

"So we went over there and he downed a triple scotch in practically one gulp. He smacked his lips and said, 'Dick, I'm ready.'"

Out in the hall, the audience had taken its place. Various estimates of the evening's attendance have been advanced over the years, ranging from about 700 to 1700. Mingus' assertion in 1975 to Ted

Photograph by Alan Scharf.

O'Reilly that the concert was "a sell out, [you] couldn't get in the door," can be safely discounted; Alex Barris' *Globe and Mail* review of the concert would put the audience at "about half the hall's capacity."

Whatever the number, the majority of the crowd must have been in the first and second balconies; a photograph of the ground floor taken soon after the concert began shows a mere scattering of fans. The audience is young, predominantly male and almost exclusively white, although four young blacks in what appear to be matching dark suits sit on the aisle eight rows back. They may be members of the Lionel Hampton Orchestra that would soon start its first set at the Colonial Tavern, just around the corner.

The hall's lights went down. Graham Topping and his 16 musicians emptied out from the wings onto the stage. First things first: the national anthem, *God Save the Queen*, was required by law at the outset or conclusion of an evening's entertainment.

One of Topping's trumpeters, Erich Traugott, a veteran of such situations, remembers that the task often fell to the American headliners, who would have next to no warning and certainly no arrangement. In such situations, they played *My Country 'Tis of Thee*, which shares its melody with *God Save the Queen*, entirely off the cuff. "It would always be a delight to the Canadian musicians to hear this – some band like Duke Ellington would go

The CBC All-Stars, Massey Hall, May 15, 1953. Trumpets (left to right): Don Johnson, Julius Piekarz, Erich Traugott, Bernie Rowe. Trombones (left to right): Ron Hughes, Ross Culley, Russ Meyers, Steve Richards. Saxophones (left to right): Julian Filanowski, Bernie Piltch, Gordie Evans, Hart Wheeler, Norman Symonds. Piano: Ralph Fraser. Bass: Howie Morris. Drums. Doug Bennett. Graham Topping, standing with the trombones, has his back to the camera. Photograph by Harold Robinson.

through a night of extremely difficult arrangements and then just murder *My Country 'Tis of Thee*."

This time, however, the Toronto musicians did the honors, and apparently to no better effect. Alone among the surviving members of the Topping band, Norm Symonds recalls, "Somebody reminded us we had to play *God Save the Queen*. There was no arrangement, so half of the band stood in a corner of the stage and played it in unison. It was very embarrassing, a horrible way to start... It unnerved us all."

Topping and his men, casual in a mix of suits, ties, sport jackets and open-neck shirts, found their places at centre stage. The saxophones played from the floor, the brass from two risers in behind. Doug Bennett sat partially obscured, his drums directly behind those of Max Roach. Topping spent the 45-minute set on his feet, conducting from the front and playing from various spots back in the sections.

Harold Robinson

Harold Robinson

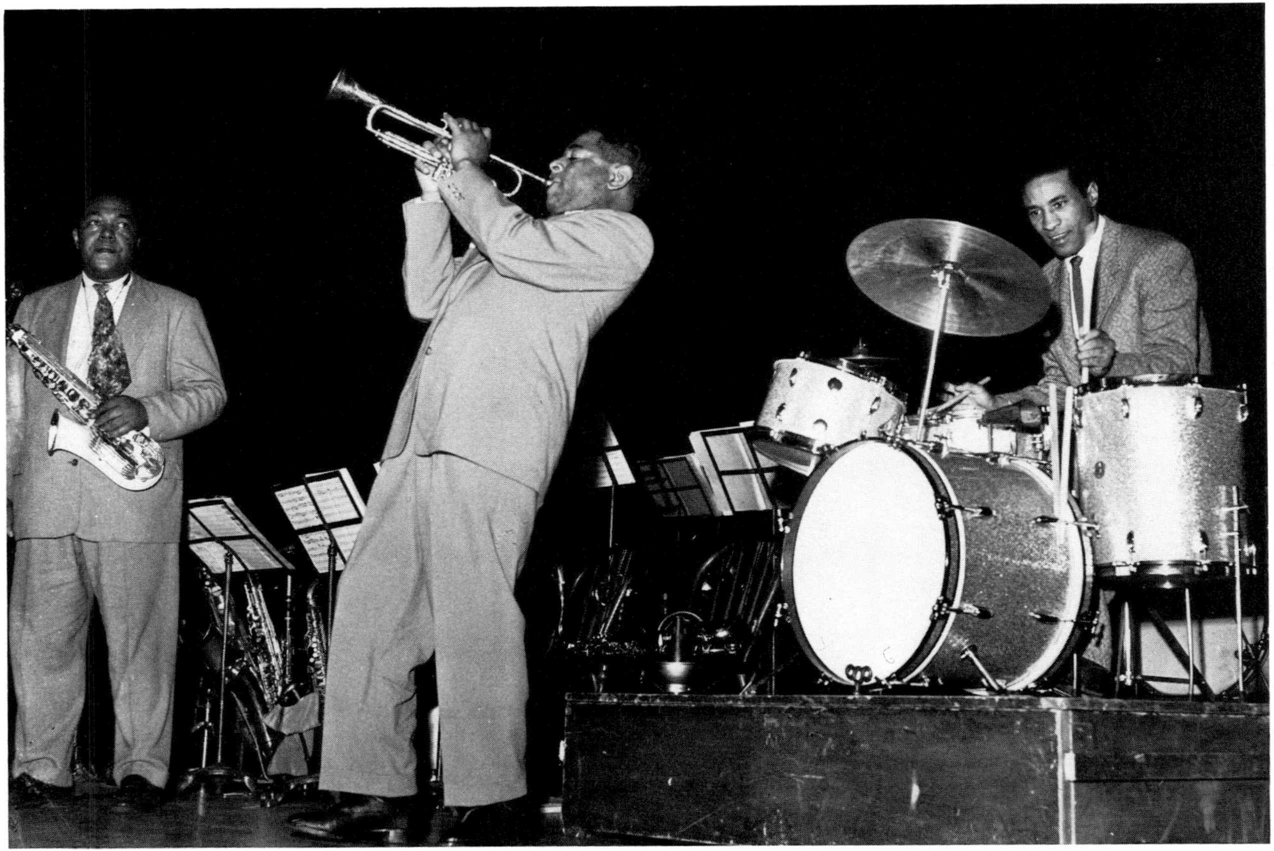

Harold Robinson

Harold Robinson

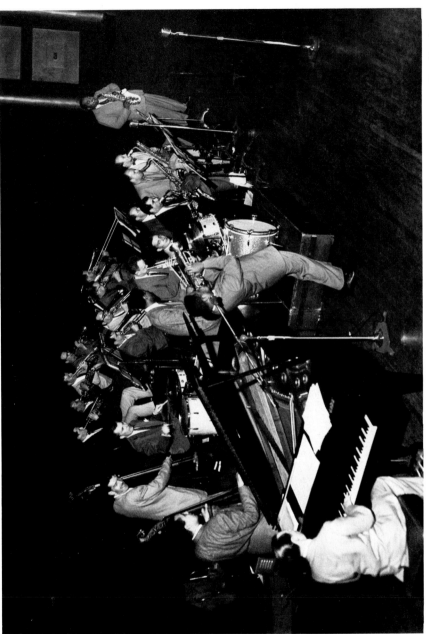

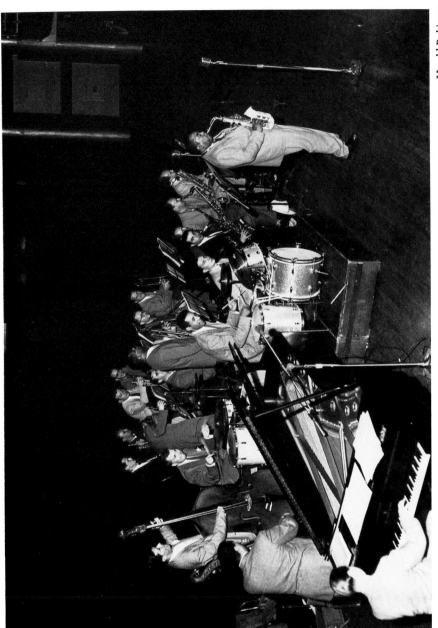

Alan Scharf

Alan Scharf

Alan Scharf

Alan Scharf

The borrowed Ampex recorder had been set up in the Massey Hall sound booth adjacent to the first balcony. Norm Speight, whose Speight Soundcraft Laboratories had handled the public address system in the hall since the late 1930s, was in charge, hidden from the audience by a curtain. A tape was running either on the Ampex or on the hall's standard recording equipment as Topping counted off a Woody Herman chart, *The Goof and I.*

Tenorman Julian Filanowski is featured first on *Goof,* followed in turn by Graham Topping and alto saxophonist Gordie Evans. Filanowski was filling in for Roy Smith, and Evans for Jerry Toth. Both Smith and Toth were among the band's main arrangers and primary soloists. Filanowski and Evans consequently would be heavily featured throughout the concert.

Evans, then 34 and four years away from joining the Sam Donahue band stateside, would remember the experience well. "God, to stand up there and have to play solos with Graham's band knowing that the people are there to hear Parker... I'll tell you, the old fingers were shaking."

The audience shows no impatience, though, and seems to have been won over by the fourth tune, *Harvard Blues,* one of two Count Basie pieces on the program. A succession of trumpet soloists, topped off by high-note man Bernie Rowe, generates an enthusiastic response that is sustained by Jerry Toth's *Mambo,* Basie's robust *Beaver Junction* and Roy Smith's ballad arrangement of *The Nearness of You* for trombonist Ross Culley.

Even Norman Symonds' difficult *Fugue for Reeds and Brass,* a very early example of the third-stream idiom that would preoccupy several Canadian composers by the late 1950s, draws a few whistles at the outset of respectful applause. The composition, written contrapuntally with no allowance for solos, is a tough read for a band playing on a single rehearsal. "Nobody," saxophonist Hart Wheeler would remember, "was looking at the audience through *that* goddamn tune!"

As if to set up the quintet, the Topping band takes out two of its bop charts, Roy Smith's *What's Shmoo?* and Gerry Mulligan's ambitious *Elevation,* the latter drawn out further by solos from

Graham Topping, trumpet, with (l to r) Steve Richards, Julian Filanowski, Bernie Piltch, Gordie Evans, Hart Wheeler (hidden) and Norman Symonds. Photograph by Harold Robinson.

pianist Ralph Fraser, Gordie Evans, Topping, Fraser again, Evans, fellow altoist Bernie Piltch, Evans for a third time, and finally Hart Wheeler. Each of the saxophonists tries hard to get a rise out of the crowd; Piltch is particularly passionate, and Wheeler's gritty, honking tenor, supported by riffs from the full band, brings the set to a shouting, JATP-like conclusion.

There were calls for more as the musicians eased back their chairs, rose slowly, stepped down and began the long walk toward the wings. Howie Morris slid his bass along the floor under the piano; the horn players set their instruments down on their chairs or propped them up on floor stands. The cheering continued for another half minute before the emcee stepped up to the mike at the front of the stage.

"Well, that's it for now. We'll be hearing from Graham a little bit later in the show. We've got some more boys to come along now..."

The "boys" had already made their presence backstage known. Voices had been raised while the Topping band was in performance. Voices raised in greeting as the New York musicians arrived one by one, suggests Erich Traugott. Voices raised in anger, suggest several other Toronto musicians.

Gordie Evans: "I never heard anything that was actually said, but I heard shouting."

Hart Wheeler: "There was *some* problem and it seemed to be a secret. The whole feeling in the air seemed to be charged, about to explode at any minute. 'Why are these guys so mad at each other?' At least *I* thought they were mad at each other."

Norman Symonds: "We were sort of amused that big-time musicians could be squabbling like the rest of us. It gave them a greater sense of humanity, to hear these angry voices backstage."

Perhaps the five visitors, now gathered together for only the first time before the concert, discovered how much each of their number was being paid. Perhaps in the absence of any rehearsal whatsoever – and in the absence of a clear leader – they had to make some quick decisions about the concert itself with no time for a consensus. Perhaps they had simply counted heads in the hall and realized their respective percentages of the "musicians' share of the net profit" would, with 15 cents, buy a cup of coffee after the show.

By the time the Toronto musicians had made their way offstage, not without some trepidation, the crisis seemed to have passed.

Indeed, Gillespie was discovered in mid-meal. He had ordered in a T-bone steak. "I don't think he had any utensils," recalls Erich Traugott, "so he just ate it holding the bone."

The senior man in the quintet, John Birks Gillespie at 35 had enjoyed the greatest popular success of any of the five musicians. It was he, not Parker, who had come to personify bebop in the public eye. Of course the trumpeter cut a colorful figure, what with, variously, his goatee, his beret, his horn-rimmed glasses, his bow ties, his bursting cheeks and his onstage antics. When *Life* ran a photo essay on bebop in October of 1948, Gillespie was front and centre; Parker, whose sartorial flare would never extend beyond florid neckwear, went unmentioned.

By 1948, though, Gillespie had moved from small, classic bop groups to the head of an orchestra given over to modern jazz with a decided Cuban flavor. The big band would last just another year or so and Gillespie's productive pace of the late 1940s began to slow. But if his career lacked for direction at the turn of the 1950s, the trumpeter himself had nevertheless seldom played better.

A rivalry of sorts had been established between Parker and Gillespie in the minds of the cognoscenti, if not in the minds of the supposed rivals themselves. After all, it was Parker who, in a 1948 *Down Beat* Blindfold Test, described Gillespie as "the other half of my heartbeat."

After their early recording sessions together in 1945 and an ill-fated trip to Los Angeles in 1946, they pursued parallel and independent careers, crossing paths on only rare occasions. The Toronto concert was perhaps the fourth such occasion since 1946; their TV appearance together in 1952 on Earl Wilson's "Stage Entrance" resulted in the only known footage extant of Parker in performance.

By the time Parker and Gillespie made their way out from the wings of Massey Hall – Bird looking rumpled in an unpressed suit and Dizzy standing dapper, not a crease out of place – they had already spent several hours in each other's company en route to Toronto. At centrestage, finally, it was Gillespie, not Parker, who took charge as a matter of course.

"All the guys respected me," the trumpeter states flatly. "I was the leader, and that was that."

Before the year was out, Gillespie would introduce the custom-made trumpet whose bell, tilted up at 45-degree angle, was to become as much a personal trademark as his ballooning cheeks. For the moment, though, he was still playing a conventional horn. He blew a few notes and probably whistled one or two more as he noticed the effect of Massey Hall's vaulted-ceiling acoustics – what Steve Richards, a trombonist in the Topping band, described as "like being in a rain barrel for a jazz man." Gillespie, remembers Richards, turned around quickly to the rhythm section and uttered an "Oh, *baby*," as if to say, "what's going to happen when we start to *swing?*"

"When we got together," Gillespie reiterates, "everybody looked to me as the leader. So I said, 'What are we going to play?' Everybody knew *Salt Peanuts*, everybody knew *A Night in Tunisia*, everybody knew whatever... so we just *rammed* into it."

In 1984, Roach recalled the same moment in similar terms. Quoted in Gillespie's *To Be or Not to Bop*, he said "... just prior to going on the bandstand, we decided what we're going to play on that particular concert. So it was pure spontaneity. That's the thing about that date. It wasn't like, 'O.K., we'll rehearse two or three hours here.' We just went onstage, and things began to happen."

Things begin to happen in a very leisurely fashion. The tune is *Perdido**, played just as Juan Tizol wrote it. There are no unspoken substitutions this time. The cognoscenti are nevertheless puzzled: this is an odd place for a meeting of bebop giants to begin. It is immediately obvious the musicians are anything but prepared for the concert.

---

* As released on record, the Massey Hall performances have been subject to some later alteration in the studio. A new bass line has been overdubbed on most tracks – in 1975, Mingus told Ted O'Reilly, "I used a different bass to get a different tone on the overdub" – and some editing has been done. *Perdido* has been issued both in its original form and with a new bass line. [See discography, p. 105fn] Mingus' brief solo *dénouement* heard on some releases of Jazz at Massey Hall is strictly a studio invention.

Moreover, Parker and Gillespie are in rather different frames of mind as they stand in front and to the left of Powell, Mingus and Roach, all five men dwarfed by the huge Massey Hall stage – 72 feet wide, 36 feet at its deepest, the ceiling a good three stories above them.

It is Parker's mood, relaxed and laconic, that sets the initial tone of *Perdido*. The six bars of the Tizol riff that survive on record are not a model of unison playing; it is Roach who catches the ear instead with a crisp Latin rhythm played on cowbell and tom. A coy, two-bar trumpet break sets up Parker's three choruses.

He is in no great hurry. His first phrase sputters slightly. There is a reflective pause of equal length and then a shorter answering line that brings some degree balance to what follows. The improvisation flows well from here on, in a reasoned and affable way. But the audience, primed by several years of JATP, is impatient for excitement, if not confrontation. Gillespie, standing to Parker's right, begins to offer vocal encouragement, echoing a laughing figure at the end of Bird's first chorus with a chuckle of his own.

The trumpeter keeps up the chatter and leads the crowd in a mild uproar halfway through the second chorus, as Parker repeats a shapely, four-note phrase, decends, and repeats it again. Without substantially altering the careful argument of his solo – he has done little more than brighten his tone slightly and sculpted a phrase with a certain deliberation – Bird nods to the crowd.

Of course the crowd, and Gillespie, are clearly caught up in their own enthusiasm. Not long into Parker's third chorus, a woman squeals sharply. The audience responds with a cheer. But nothing in Bird's playing would warrant such a response. The joke is visual. Gillespie is no doubt up to tricks.

Parker immediately begins to wind down, sounding briefly distracted – perhaps disheartened to find that the trumpeter's antics are at least as well appreciated as his own artistry. He bows out of his solo with exactly the same keening phrase that he had played at the conclusion of *Wahoo* with Brew Moore on Montreal television four months before.

Gillespie picks up on the phrase at the outset of his four choruses. For the moment, he sustains Bird's measured pace, quoting *Laura* –

and perhaps thereby taunting Parker, who had recorded the tune with strings – much to the amusement of the audience. By the middle of his first chorus, however, the trumpeter is blowing harder and begins to mix the brash rhetoric and quick melodic invention that characterizes his playing throughout the evening.

This is what the crowd has come to hear and the response is quick, both out in the hall and from the stage. Roach, who had been so subdued behind Parker, picks up Gillespie's bolder patterns and throws their rhythms back at the trumpeter, setting up a bump-and-grind backbeat at the outset of the third chorus that seems to suit the proceedings perfectly. After Parker's reasoned statement, Gillespie's solo seems a scattered, though entirely effective creation, with its squealing, valved effects, the occasional quote (his own *Birks Works*, for example, at the end of the third chorus) and those easily-targeted high notes that would have the JATP veterans at Massey Hall thinking of Roy Eldridge.

The presence of an audience seems neither here nor there to Bud Powell, whose three, tidy, self-absorbed choruses pass without audible distraction or, for that matter, noticeable response. Gillespie leads Parker back into the ensemble and the two men drift rather aimlessly until Roach's eight-bar solo propels them bodily – the trumpeter at least – into the Tizol theme. Gillespie screeches dramatically on a high note as Parker simply repeats the tune's three-note riff.

Much has been made of Parker's reference to Gillespie as "my worthy constituent" in his introduction to the trumpeter's *Salt Peanuts*. ("At this time we would like to play a tune that was composed by my worthy constituent, Mr. Dizzy Gillespie, in the year of 1942...") It is significant, however, that the remark survives on record out of context, preceded and followed as it is by an edit. Parker could choose his words carefully for effect. It would appear that the record's producers also chose Parker's words carefully – perhaps even irresponsibly. Those who hear irony dripping from the remark would find further support for the scenario that the two men were in conflict.

Salt Peanuts, played at an exceedingly fast tempo, has been preserved on record with at least two other edits within the body of the performance*. The tune begins in a rush as Roach starts a fast tattoo on an open sock cymbal for two bars and then rolls and kicks for two bars more. The horn arrangement is played from memory with problematic results; Gillespie and Parker had recorded the tune together for Guild eight years before, virtually to the day, under the trumpeter's name. A splice immediately preceding Gillespie's vocal appears to have cleaned up some sort of small disaster.

Parker again takes the first solo, a pattern that would stand throughout the evening. If his description of Gillespie moments before was in fact pointed, the trumpeter has not been in the least chastened. Gillespie carries on shouting "salt peanuts... salt peanuts, salt peanuts... salt *pea*nuts... salt *peanuts*..." further and further off mike during the initial 16 bars of Bird's first chorus. It is one of the concert's truly electrifying moments. Parker seems to play off Gillespie's verbal interjections. Roach is driving fiercely – his contribution to the concert cannot be underestimated – and Parker sustains the intensity for two brisk choruses before winding down in the third.

The performance stalls on the handover to Gillespie, as usual taking the second solo, but he wastes little time in getting back up to speed and matches Bird for excitement if not for pure invention. The audience has quietened; Gillespie need no longer play to the house and even his most ostentatious ideas are integrated into the three choruses of what would prove one of his strongest improvisations of the evening.

It is Powell who takes the extra chorus this time. Deservedly so: it is a wild, heedless invention, played at the edge without a slip. Gillespie and Parker seem unimpressed, however, as they carry on a conversation at one point during that fourth chorus; the recording further robs Powell of his due by splicing his last phrase directly onto the first strokes of a long Roach solo. Gillespie and Parker, at least temporarily reconciled, are both heard on the final, hiccuped "Salt *Pea*nuts, Salt *Pea*nuts."

---

* This is the only quintet performance from Massey Hall with the original bass line intact on all releases.

All the Things You Are is both the concert's ballad, more or less, and its curio, most certainly. Gillespie is remembered to have peered quizzically under the raised piano lid at Powell during the evening; he would certainly have been justified in looking askance in the course of this particular performance.

After the various discourtesies shown Powell during *Salt Peanuts*, this may just be "Bud's Revenge." Parker and Gillespie give the tune a non-committal reading, using Parker's decending, three-note *Bird of Paradise* figure to set up to the Jerome Kern theme, as had become – and remains – common practice. Once Parker steps forward, Powell undertakes and holds resolutely to a pedestrian rhythmic pattern of chords whose harmonic extensions have the effect of blurring the changes and squeezing out the soloist. Back to the wall, Parker squirms uncomfortably through his initial eight bars, ending with whimper of submission – to no avail.

He squirms a little more, then quotes *The Kerry Dance* in search of room to move – Gillespie laughs sympathetically; *he* gets the point, even if Powell apparently doesn't. Parker plays off the melody, he works against the changes. Finally he gives up the struggle, relaxes and turns quietly lyrical in his second 36-bar chorus. His brief reference to *On the Trail* may be an affirmation of bearings established, but he is never entirely settled nor out of trouble.

Gillespie sees the merits of Parker's understated approach, screws in a mute and begins to blow softly and move quickly. Powell is generally less obstructive rhythmically, but his changing harmonies still leave some of Gillespie's longer lines twisting awkwardly at centre stage. Gillespie is, however, more consistent than Parker, if again less gripping at his most reponsive to Powell's challenge.

Perhaps perversely, the pianist's own solo is quite circumspect, indeed the very model of innocence, and gives way diplomatically to Mingus after just a single chorus*. The bassist, who had followed Powell dutifully behind Parker and Gillespie, gets his first solo of the night, 36 cautious bars with the two horns blowing softly behind, in effect breathing down his neck.

---

* *All the Things You Are* has been issued on record both in its original form and with a new bass line overdubbed. In the dubbed version, the original line can still be distinguished at various points during Mingus' solo.

Parker introduces the *Bird of Paradise* figure that signals the return of the Kern melody. He then takes the initiative for the first time in the concert, cutting into Gillespie's closing cadenza with the familiar *52nd Street Theme*, as if to call an intermission or at least to put a strong finish on what had been a troubled performance. Powell catches the cue immediately and doubles the horns at several points in the familiar arrangement, but continues on alone at the piano, crashing further and further into discord as the other musicians stop playing and, no doubt, begin to look around the stage for the nearest exit.

Intermission lasted a long three-quarters of an hour. There were more words backstage. According to Roach, Mingus was somewhat in the dark when it came to the tacit arrangements that 52nd Street veterans played in each other's company – "for example, the arrangement of *Salt Peanuts* is kind of tricky, the breaks in it, and we went into it without rehearsal. Mingus was peeved, naturally...

"We asked Mingus why he was puffed up, and he said, 'Well, man, you guys are just going your own sweet way and forgetting about the fact that I'm from the West Coast.'

"We said, 'Oh, shit... we didn't mean to...' And that was that: it was all about music."

The CBLT telecast of the Marciano/Walcott fight was set to start at 10. Fans and musicians alike streamed across Shuter Street to the Silver Rail to watch as many rounds as they could before the concert resumed. Dawdlers who stopped outside Massey Hall to take in the cool, clear night air would miss the fight altogether: Jersey Joe, clearly the musicians' choice, lasted two minutes and 25 seconds into the first round, scarcely a half minute longer than Parker's solo on *Perdido*. Walcott would receive $250,000 for his efforts. Marciano, who had opted for 30% of the gross receipts, took home $166,000.

Gordie Evans spent most of the break out in the alley on the west side of Massey Hall in the company of his girl friend, a Toronto model. Gillespie, who knew the saxophonist from previous visits to Toronto, joined them at one point, clowning around and displaying a particular interest in Evans' companion. As if playing on the same stage as Charlie Parker wasn't enough for one night, Evans muses, "I had Dizzy after my girl."

The NJS's Gary Dutton encountered Powell backstage and made a request for *Un Poco Loco*, a tune that the pianist had first recorded just two years before. "Don't play that no more, man," Powell mumbled, continuing on his way. "Don't play that..."

Parker, according to a later published report, had found his way to a bar in the King Edward Hotel, a five-minute walk south on Victoria Street. There (wrote Jack Batten in *Saturday Night* in 1978) "he downed two more triples and fell into a brawl with a fellow drinker. He returned to the hall rather the worse for wear, with one pocket ripped out of his suit jacket..." It may or may not be an indication of the story's veracity that a photograph taken of Parker later in the evening shows his jacket to be intact.

Intermission dragged on with no sign of an end. With the fight over so quickly, the fans – if not the musicians – had drifted back to the hall and were growing restless. In the continuing absence of the others, Gary Dutton recalls, Roach took to the stage alone.

At 28, he was the youngest member of the quintet (three and a half months Powell's junior) and, by all accounts, the most responsible. Not the first of the bop drummers, but in short order the most influential, he had played with Parker and Gillespie as a teenager and was present at 20 on Parker's first Savoy session in November 1945. He was subsequently a member of Parker's working quintet from 1947 to 49 and had often played in Powell's trio. By 1953 both a business and musical associate of Mingus, he was, as much as any one of the five musicians, the link figure in the quintet.

Sitting spotlit at his drums on the darkened stage, he began an extended solo that would come to be called *Drum Conversation*.

Earl (Bud) Powell, also 28, had been in and out of New York mental hospitals since 1947. Notwithstanding his incapacitation, and its interruptive effect on his career, he exerted a primary influence on bop piano. His finest improvisations had an energy, control and imagination that often belied, indeed defied, his condition.

Dick Wattam remembers Powell as "the picture of calm confidence" at Massey Hall, but Alan Scharf suggests, "It was amazing that he could play: he wasn't 'with' us most of the time there... Bud was mostly 'unconscious.' You could usually see the whites of his eyes. It was just amazing."

It was perhaps also just a little deceptive. At one point, several NJS members were in Powell's company in a hotel room. Scharf continues, "Somebody casually said, 'Who wrote *Lullaby of Birdland*?' Immediately, he perked right up and said, 'George Shearing,' and then he went right back. So he was listening..."

And came time – twice led carefully out onstage by Oscar Goodstein, slumping at the Steinway, righting himself somewhat casually off-centre, cocking his head this way and that, twisting his feet under the piano bench or to one side of the pedals and turning his ankles over impossibly, in sum a Cubist figure of unlikely angles – he played.

With *Drum Conversation* complete, Powell and Mingus join Roach for a trio set of six or seven tunes. Taken together, the performances are something of a Powell retrospective. Three are typical of Powell's exhilarating, uptempo bop style – Ray Noble's *Cherokee*, Shearing's *Lullaby of Birdland* and Mingus' *Jubilee*, the first two presented on record in excerpted form.

Cherokee fades in as Powell drifts toward a somewhat equivocal reading of the theme, almost oblivious to the resolve in Roach's brush and bass drum work. Taken at the fastest tempo of the three bop pieces, it is the most linear of Powell's solos in the set. But the pace has its effect: his phrases trail off as often as they follow through cleanly one to the next. As a result, there is a rather free, perhaps even lost quality to the improvisation, which is nevertheless kept on course by the drive generated by Mingus and Roach. A drum solo appears to have been scissored neatly into this performance on record, or least cleaned up around the edges; there is applause for a particularly furious brush passage partway through, but none, curiously, at the end.

Lullaby is a shorter, though stealthier piano improvisation with just the occasional falter. On record, it begins in mid-solo and works its way quickly to the Shearing theme. Powell sustains a high level of invention throughout, his playing a shade more relaxed and certainly more coherent at the marginally slower tempo.

Jubilee in turn is a particularly clean, cogent performance, as strong, balanced and well-recorded a trio piece as any of the three uptempo items, benefiting from the more melodically-developed, left-hand punctuation that draws out the prebop influences in his playing. Roach's sly fours lie naturally in the performance – there are only brushes, no scissors, here.

George Gershwin's *Embraceable You* and Cole Porter's *I've Got You Under My Skin* turned up in many of Powell's performances during the first, post-Creedmore months. Each had a set arrangement and reflected the decorative influence of Art Tatum. Powell descends suddenly into *Embraceable You*, blocking out the chords of the piece firmly, at times heavily, introducing some ornamentation and arpeggiation in the Tatum manner but maintaining a deliberate hand throughout. It is the very antithesis of his feverish attack at faster tempos.

The effect is forlorn, a mere memory. Mingus told Ted O'Reilly in 1975: "Actually, some kids in the audience were crying when Bud was playing *Embraceable You*. I could see the tears in their eyes..." Mingus paused, adding melodramatically, "besides my own."

I've Got You Under My Skin moves uncertainly atop a Spanish figure repeated by Mingus, but Powell gives the piece a fairly straight ballad interpretation to the point of taking 16 florid bars, unaccompanied and out of tempo. Roach brushes a Latin figure very softly against his snare drum, leaving the louder snap of Mingus' shoe leather on the wood stage to mark time in this stilted performance, perhaps the least consequential of the set. It was not included in the initial Debut release.

The shouts of "More!" that follow *Sure Thing* on record indicate that the piece is played at or near the end of the set, perhaps as an encore. Cited in the December 1953 issue of *Metronome* with *Bassically Speaking** as the highpoints of the original Debut release, it

---

* *Bass-ically Speaking*, an extended feature for Mingus, may also have been played at Massey Hall, but is represented on record by a later studio version.

was described as "a masterpiece... a kind of modern Toccata, like Bach's 'touchpieces' in its unfolding of pianistic resources." It is, indeed, a very proper presentation of Powell's classical inclinations. The Jerome Kern melody is offered lightly and dryly in a contrapuntal fashion. Development is limited, however, and in retrospect the piece seems more interesting for what it represents than what it is.

Parker and Gillespie have been offstage for a good 75 minutes and, according to some accounts, have had to be cajoled out of the Silver Rail for the second set. They seem no worse for the interval. Nor for the disappointment – with head hung low, and forearm across his eyes in mock despair, Gillespie breaks the news of Jersey Joe's fate to the Massey Hall audience.

Their opening salvo on Denzil Best's *Wee**, an *I Got Rhythm* variant known alternatively as *Allen's Alley* (after tenorman Allan Eager), startles with its suddenness. The tempo is comparable to that for *Salt Peanuts*. This time, though, Parker is on the offensive from the first note and meets Gillespie aggressively on the bridge. His solo is charged with confidence; his tone is bold, even quarrelsome, and his phrases are clipped by their own urgency.

The scuffles of *All The Things You Are* are long behind him. Powell is now in control at the piano. The footing secure, Parker swings hard, even fiercely, and his enthusiastic swashbuckling takes him past the end of his third chorus and a few bars into Gillespie's first. The trumpeter responds by adding a fourth chorus to his own solo. The audience is again alive, and Gillespie's playing, now choppy and only roughly articulated at the same extreme tempo that Parker has just handled so smoothly, is nevertheless sufficiently sophistic to excite the crowd even further.

Powell, primed by his own set, also takes four choruses, each more intense – more physical, more headlong – than the last, building to a level that only Roach, of the other musicians, could sustain. The Best theme once again makes a dramatic entry after the

* The first eight bars of *Wee* do not survive on record. All releases of the performance on record have an overdubbed bass line.

drummer's three choruses, and Parker holds sway over Gillespie on the bridge – a final triumph.

Gillespie sounds suitably abashed as he announces Tadd Dameron's *Hot House*. Roach again kicks the piece off, this time at an easy swing. Parker and Gillespie take up the melody in a perfunctory manner; they had previously recorded the tune together in May of 1945 during the same Guild session that produced *Salt Peanuts*. Gillespie, further to the fore on the recording than Parker, is less than precise with the descending Dameron line. It is an enticing melody, and Parker, Gillespie and Powell each devote some small part of their improvisation to a simple paraphrase.

Parker remains off mike for most of his solo, moving in closer only at the end of the second of his three choruses. The distant sound of his alto underlines his offhand start to the solo itself. Still, it has the design, direction and, eventually, the dynamic that Parker intuitively introduced into each of his improvisations, no matter how abrupt some of the component phrases, nor how unlikely in this instance the "Habanera" quote from *Carmen*. The swoop, angularity and occasional stridency of Parker's playing on *Hot House* begin to anticipate the way in which Eric Dolphy would personalize his influence.

The slower tempo is kinder to Gillespie than the bristling pace of *Wee* had been. With renewed articulation, he gives his three choruses a thoughtful and generally serious tone that is challenged once by his reprise of Parker's quote from *Carmen* and once more by a reference to *Laura* that rightly passes without notice this second time around. It is almost as though Parker has finally redefined the concert's aesthetic; Gillespie continues to be a vocal bystander, but both he and the Toronto audience have come to find greater value in the purely musical.

In this, perhaps Powell also deserves some credit. Once again his solo is measured, balanced and entirely without conceit. The five musicians ease back to the *Hot House* line after Powell's third chorus. Comes the bridge, though, Mingus strikes out on his own. With Roach's ride and sock cymbals at a whisper, the bassist feints briefly at Dameron's secondary theme and then plays on against the tune's changes. In other company the solo might seem a supple invention. Following Parker, Gillespie and Powell, it simply seems sturdy*.

Someone stomps a foot firmly to the stage toward the end of his second chorus, perhaps mocking the sharp, unsteady sound of Mingus' tapping toe. There is laughter. Parker and Gillespie each fidget with their horns before slipping back in at the end for a single repeat of the Dameron line. The transition seems agreeable enough, but Mingus would later make known that it was not at all to his liking.

"And now," Gillespie informs the audience, "we would like to play *Ce soir en Tunis – A Night in Tunisia.*" Mingus and Roach set up the rhythm, the bassist introducing the tune's familiar, eight-note ostinato and the drummer playing a counter pattern first on cowbell and then on cymbal**. Parker ghosts the bass line and Gillespie exercises his prerogative as the tune's composer, taking the counter-melody, demurely muted, for himself. It is the second Gillespie tune of the concert; Parker's compositions have gone unrepresented.

A Night in Tunisia is a long-winded piece, what with its rhythm shift, its various cross and counter themes and its final set-up riff. Parker seems to be chafing. He gives notice of some impatience on the bridge, dispensing with the second half of Gillespie's composed line in favor of a mad, melodic dash of his own invention, and then follows the riff section with a majestic, four-bar break that draws an appreciative cheer from the audience.

There's a certain swagger to the three Parker choruses that follow. The tempo is right, and he is off to as good a start as he has made all night. A little too good, as it turns out. His solo does not – cannot, perhaps – match the grace, balance or simple purity of the break. It remains an inspired improvisation, but fragments almost immediately into short, nattering, high-cornered figures that are spaced but not necessarily connected by longer, lyrical lines. No less than any of his other solos on the night, it is a highly charged, changeable piece of work, expressively responsive to the whim, the

exhilaration and the distraction of the moment. No two of his solos
have been alike emotionally; any two successive choruses would be
only slightly more uniform.

If, in the same respect, Gillespie has at times been no less exciting,
he has been less excitable. He takes three choruses on *A Night in
Tunisia*, finishing the evening with 20 to Powell's 18 and Parker's
17; of course on laughs he would wind up ahead by an even wider
margin. This time, his solo is precise, shapely and, once into the second chorus with a word of encouragement from Parker, increasingly punchy in a way that would have fans thinking again of Roy
Eldridge.

The stoic Powell stays in character with three firm choruses of his
own and appears to skid right past the ensemble's return. The quintet fashions its final cadence after a single repeat of the tune's main
theme, Gillespie soaring in the lead. Powell, however, isn't quite finished: as the ovation begins to swell, he can be heard again launch-
ing a slow descent into dissonance, signalling – as he had on *52nd
Street Theme* – the conclusion of the set.

As the quintet neared the end of its set, Graham Topping's musicians began to gather backstage. Julian Filanowski had been listening all along from the wings, but Ralph Fraser had taken a seat in
the front row, the better to watch Bud Powell. Gordie Evans stood
on the ground floor against a side wall, while Hart Wheeler had
wandered around the hall before sitting down in the first balcony.

There would be three more numbers by the Topping band, *Lover
Come Back to Me* as lifted from Les Brown by Roy Smith, Russ
Meyers' *Just Where You Are* and Julius Piekarz' *Mambo Macocoa*.
Topping, Gordie Evans and Ralph Fraser bravely took their solos in
the New York musicians' long shadows.

Whether by pre-arrangement or on the spur of the moment,
Parker, Gillespie, Mingus and Roach then joined the Topping band
for a finale. Little survives of the encounter save for several photographs of the two bands onstage together. Hart Wheeler remembers Gillespie standing at the end of the saxophone section and
laughing wildly. The trumpeter had been in high spirits all night, of
course, but Wheeler's hometown insecurity allowed for another

Max Roach, Graham Topping, Julian Filanowski, Dizzy Gillespie, Charlie Parker. Photograph by Alan Scharf.

interpretation. "I thought, 'God, are we really *that* bad?'"

The 21 musicians probably played a blues – possibly Tiny Kahn's *Tiny's Blues*, suggest Wheeler and Evans. In truth the details have been all but forgotten. Ralph Fraser, who was at the piano for Parker and Gillespie as they took their final solos of the concert, nevertheless remembers the moment's larger significance. "Not too many people, in Toronto anyway, can say that they played with Charlie Parker. Lots of people played with Dizzy, but Charlie didn't last that long after that, did he?"

Some 20 minutes after the concert, the hall was empty. Mingus was playing the Steinway on the darkened stage. Parker stood nearby on the main floor of the hall, smoking a cigaret. His suit was soaked with sweat, but he appeared relaxed; he is remembered to have inquired about the possibility of sitting in somewhere else that night. Alan Scharf, carrying his camera and flash, approached. "I remember saying, 'Charlie, may I take your picture?' Much to my surprise, Mingus, who was sitting at the piano, answered... So I had to take his picture first, then I took Bird's."

Backstage, there were still more words. Mingus told Mike Hennessey in 1971, "I remember complaining to Dizzy that there were no bass solos on any of the numbers, and he got wild and violent." Of course Mingus had played two solos. Gillespie recalls the circumstances of the second, on *Hot House*. "Mingus went to play a little longer. I came in a little too quickly. I think maybe he wanted to play three choruses, instead of two. It was one of those things. There was a word said."

The bassist's mood would not improve. A friendly inquiry later in the evening from the NJS' Roger Feather about the tapes of the concert brought a decidedly unfriendly reply. "He gave me a ferocious look," Feather told Jack Batten in 1978, "and he said, 'They're *mine*, white boy.' And he clutched them tighter."

Several meetings followed in the next few hours. The first, between the New York musicians and members of the New Jazz Society, took place in a basement room at Massey Hall.

There, likely to no one's great surprise, Dick Wattam revealed the NJS's shortfall in funds. After the taxman had taken a cut off the top at the box office, and after Graham Topping had received $450, there wasn't enough money left to cover the balance owing the quintet. "I personally was just mortified," Wattam recalls. "I just wanted the floor to swallow me up."

Reactions to the news varied. Roach describes himself as "fairly cool. My sobriety was always there. I just said, 'Well, so be it.'"

He remembers Parker speaking up. "Bird said, 'Turn out the lights.' So naturally we all looked at each other and thought, 'Now what? *Now* what?' Many years later, I began to think about that. Remember those old Charlie Chan pictures? The lights would go out, and when the lights came back on, somebody would be dead."

Others recall that Parker – who had, according to Wattam, *already* received his $200 by way of an advance – protested that his responsibilities to a wife and children made payment absolutely essential. Still others suggest that Parker did in fact become violent.

It was also at this meeting that the existence of the tapes became general knowledge. "Don't worry about the money right now," Wattam told the musicians. "The concert has been recorded and it's worth *thousands*."

Parker again protested, this time reminding those present – as he had in Montreal – of his exclusive contract with Mercury Records.

Another group of NJS members gathered somewhat self-consciously for what had been planned as a post-concert celebration at a nearby restaurant. Boyd Raeburn was in the party. "The waiters kept saying, 'Well, should we start serving?' And nobody wanted to say 'Yes,' because they didn't want to get stuck with the bill. Eventually we said, 'Sorry...' And they said, 'Well, that's all right, it's already been paid for...'"

A third meeting followed around 3 in the morning at radio station CKFH, a short walk north on Yonge Street. The station was off the air for the night, but Mingus, Wattam, Alan Scharf and Boyd Raeburn gained entry and played back the tapes of the concert.

It was immediately apparent that Mingus, who had been so central to the recording in the first place, was the one musician in the quintet whose playing had not been properly captured on tape. According to Wattam, "Mingus nearly exploded. You couldn't hear his bass at *all*."

Mingus took final possession of the tapes then and there. Scharf later suggested in a letter published in *Saturday Night* that the bassist's first instinct was to destroy them. Wattam, Scharf wrote, immediately fired off a telegram to Barry Ulanov, editor of *Metronome*.

It read:

"DO NOT LET MINGUS ERASE TAPES. STOP. DO NOT LET MINGUS ERASE TAPES. STOP. HE IS UNBALANCED."

Cheques were issued to the musicians at still another meeting on Saturday morning. Mingus insisted on cash under the threat of selling his bass and thereby forcing the NJS to forfeit the customs bond it had posted for the instrument. He was paid by Boyd Raeburn.

Parker was spotted later by Alan Scharf at the Royal York Hotel. "He was walking around with an 'NSF' cheque. And *I* knew it was 'NSF.'

He asked a couple of questions about the 'Wattam Trucking Company'
– somebody had misled him there – and he was going over to cash it."

Parker finally wound up at Premier Radio, which had sold tickets
for the NJS and had been listed in the newspaper ads for the concert. The owner, a jazz fan, agreed to cash the cheque. He is said to
have subsequently garnisheed the wages of the NJS' treasurer and
later had the cheque framed and hung over the counter in the store.

Gillespie, meanwhile, would wait until he returned to New York
to cash his cheque. "It bounced, and bounced, and bounced like a
rubber ball..."

The musicians were back in New York – Mingus with his tapes,
Gillespie with his cheque – and the NJS members were back at
work, or in school as the case may be, when Alex Barris' review of
the concert appeared in *The Globe and Mail* the following Monday.
His remarks would take on added significance as the basis of a
report that ran in August 1953 issue of *Metronome* – the first news
the jazz world had of the Massey Hall concert.

Under headline, "Home Talent Holds Own With U.S. Jazz
Stars," Barris set the tone of his *Globe* review in his second sentence:
"By 11:30 when the boys called it quits, the score read a few scattered hits, some interesting runs by visiting pianist Bud Powell, and
a number of errors by both sides."

Barris directed his highest praise to Powell's trio set – to "Bud's
brilliant coherent playing as well as the flawless drumming of
Roach and the precise bass playing of Mingus."

Parker and Gillespie were described as "deposed bop kings" who
"rarely approached the exciting heights their works of some years ago
achieved." The trumpeter could hide behind his "comedian's mask,"
Barris wrote, but Parker "had to be content with occasionally releasing a
torrent of unrelated notes in an attempt to dazzle the crowd."

Barris took a softer line on the Topping band, whose contribution to the evening "was in some ways more substantial." He began
his final summation with a comment that the passing years would
prove ironic.

"All in all," he wrote, "it was neither a great concert nor a bad
one."

Epilogue (I)

Charlie Parker returned to the Latin Quarter in October of 1953. The Mountain Street club had just initiated a new policy with New York jazz musicians. Parker was the third to play the Quarter, following Johnny Hodges and Earl Hines.

Bird was to receive $1250 for seven nights' work, beginning on the 12th. His band was completed by four other New York musicians, trumpeter Benny (*Wahoo*) Harris, pianist Harry Biss, bassist Conrad Henry and drummer Art Mardigan.

An ad in the *Herald* for Tuesday, the 13th read:

A History-Making
Musical Jazz Event
Don't Miss
The "Bird"!
Charlie
"Bird"
Parker
and his band

An ad in the *Herald* for the 14th, however, announced that Earl Hines was "Held Over By Popular Demand."

After Parker's first night, Monday, a protest had been filed with the Montreal local of the American Federation of Musicians by the

Latin Quarter, apparently on the grounds that the club was expect-
ing a "set band" rather than what was obviously a pickup outfit. Biss,
in particular, was "always in a fog," according to Morton Berman,
the club's secretary-treasurer. At one point the Montreal pianist Art
Roberts sat in.

Parker declined the Latin Quarter's offer to stay on alone with
his old boss, Hines, and instead filed a claim with the union against
the club for outstanding wages, a sum of $743.04.

Letters (reprinted in *To Bird with Love*) followed to Leo
Cluesman, secretary of the New York local. One, from Morton
Berman on November 13, answered Parker's claim with various
charges of misrepresentation and unprofessional conduct on the
saxophonist's part, including a reference to the chewing and spitting
of lemon peels onstage "in full view of customers."

Parker's reply, four typed pages in length, dated November 18,
was well-presented and not unreasonable – the lemons were for his
stomach condition, he argued, without explaining the manner in
which he disposed of the peels – but it was ultimately deemed
unconvincing. The union ruled the following March 29 in favor of
the Latin Quarter.

In his point-by-point refutation of Berman's complaints, Parker
observed that the club was new to jazz. The Hodges and Hines bands
of the preceding two weeks played "an excellent brand of jazz [.]
entirely different from the type my orchestra plays." Berman, he
suggested, had made the unwitting comparison and found Parker's
bebop wanting.

Parker was not unsympathetic.

"However," he concluded, "this is only due to the fact that my
type of music has not appeared in Montreal too often..."

Epilogue (II)

There were three more Jazz Workshop presentations at the Chez Paree in 1953: trombonist Kai Winding on March 21, trumpeter Pete Candoli, pianist Mel Powell and bassist Max Wayne (all travelling with the Chez's evening attraction, singer Peggy Lee, who also put in an appearance) on May 16, and trumpeter Herbie Spanier (then working at Belmont Park with Benny Louis' band out of Toronto) on June 20.

Paul Bley, however, directed the Workshop's more immediate attention to the new activity upstairs at the Video Café. Brew Moore, Dick Garcia and Ted Paskert remained in town for a few days – *Down Beat*'s Montreal correspondent Henry Whiston called the trip "ill fated" in his March 25 column, adding "their proposed date lasted only five days" – but Sonny Rollins arrived on the 16th for six nights, followed on the 23rd by another tenor player, Allen Eager. Kai Winding, altoist Jackie McLean and drummer Art Taylor played the Workshop in March, followed by flutist Sam Most in early April.

By the summer, the Workshop's lease with the café had expired, funds had dwindled, and the Workshop itself had fallen victim both to internal bickering and to external disputes with the Emanon Jazz Society. Bley, it seemed, was operating as a committee of one. "There was one major player in Buzzy Bley's endeavours," remembers an Emanon principal, "and that was Buzzy Bley."

The pianist was briefly active at the Cavendish and Hale Hakala cafés before returning to New York to make his first album, with no less than Charles Mingus and Art Blakey as sidemen, for the bassist's Debut label in late November.

The Jazz Workshop had lasted scarcely a year. Meanwhile, its CBFT namesake had an even shorter life. It went off the air February 26, just three weeks after the Parker telecast.

After the Massey Hall concert, the New Jazz Society of Toronto was, Dick Wattam admits, "on its uppers there for a while." Nevertheless, the society eventually produced a few more concerts of local significance.

The Norm Amadio Trio, for example, was presented with Herbie Spanier and others at the Canadian Legion Auditorium on College Street, January 28, 1954. Norm Symonds' Octet with singer Anne Marie Moss appeared at Victoria Auditorium, a stone's throw south of Massey Hall, April 13. During the same period, the US bop pianist Al Haig played a private concert for NJS members at Melody Mill, a musicians' rooming house on Jarvis Street.

By 1955, however, the NJS was effectively inactive. Dick Wattam would continue intermittently as an agent, using a photo of Parker, Gillespie *et al* at Massey Hall as the graphic on his letterhead.

Bird returned to Massey Hall with Dizzy Gillespie on February 11, 1954 as part of the touring Festival of Modern Jazz headlined by the Stan Kenton Orchestra and the Erroll Garner Trio. Parker's playing was deemed "a bit better than on his last appearance here" by Alex Barris in *The Globe and Mail* of February 12. The concert, which also featured June Christy, Lee Konitz and Candido, was sold out.

Discography

The following abbreviations have been used in this discography:
as (alto saxophone), b (bass), bs (baritone saxophone), d (drums), g
(guitar), p (piano), tpt (trumpet), trb (trombone) and ts (tenor saxophone).

I/CBFT's "JAZZ WORKSHOP"
CBC studios, 1425 Dorchester Blvd., Montreal, 5 Feb 1953, 8:30-9
p.m. Don Cameron, emcee*

Paul Bley (p), Neil Michaud (b), Ted Paskert (d)
Jumpin' with Symphony Sid   unissued
's Wonderful   unissued

add Dick Garcia (g)
Johann Sebastian Bop   unissued

add Charlie Parker (as)
Cool Blues   Jazz Showcase 5003**

Brew Moore (ts) replaces Parker
Bernie's Tune   Jazz Showcase 5003

Parker replaces Moore
   Don't Blame Me   Jazz Showcase 5003

add Moore
   Wahoo
   [announced as *Perdido*]   Jazz Showcase 5003

II/CHEZ PAREE
1258 Stanley St., Montreal, 7 Feb 1953, about 4:30 p.m. Don
Cameron, emcee

Charlie Parker (as), Valdo Williams (p), Dick Garcia (g)
Hal Gaylor (b), Billy Graham (d)
   Ornithology   Jazz Showcase 5003/
                                              Atlantis ATS 12***

   Cool Blues   unissued

Parker, Garcia, Steep Wade (p), Bob Rudd (b), Bobby Malloy
(d)****
   Moose the Mooche   unissued

   Embraceable You   Jazz Showcase 5003

   Now's the Time   unissued

---

*The kinescope of "Jazz Workshop" with Charlie Parker has not been found. A search made in 1983 by discographer Jack Litchfield at the CBC Montreal archives led to a file card for the "Jazz Workshop" kines marked *détruits* – "destroyed." New efforts in 1989 failed to find even the file card.
**Jazz Showcase 5003 was issued under the title *Bird on the Road*.
***Atlantis ATS 12 was issued under the title *The Bird Flies Deep*.
****Various sources, including Jack Litchfield's *Canadian Jazz Discography 1916-80* and Keith White's unpublished memoir *Noting the Scene*, place the change of accompanists one tune later, between *Moose the Mooche* and *Embraceable You*. On the evidence of the surviving recording made at the Chez Paree by Bert Joss, it seems more likely for two reasons that the break preceded *Moose the Mooche*. This is consistent with (unpublished) notes about the concert made later by Len Dobbin.
   There is obviously a different drummer on *Moose the Mooche* than on *Cool Blues*, a point confirmed in January of 1989 by one of the two drummers involved, Bill Graham, on hearing

the tape. It seems implausible that Parker would dismiss, and thereby embarrass, a single musician in the middle of the set.

Moreover, there is an interruption on the Joss tape between *Cool Blues* and *Moose the
Mooche* – ie. where the break occurred – but there is *no* interruption between *Moose the
Mooche* and *Embraceable You*. This in fact is the only place on the tape where one tune runs
into the next *without* a break. Indeed, only 25 seconds elapse from the last notes of *Moose the
Mooche*, through Parker's comments (see p. 50), to the count-off for *Embraceable You*, scarce-
ly long enough for an unobtrusive change of accompanists.

Consider, too, the tempos of the tunes: *Embraceable You* is Parker's only ballad of the
afternoon and, as such, would more likely have been placed in the middle rather than than at
the start of the second set. Finally, in view of Wade's role as Parker's connection a few hours
earlier, *Moose the Mooche* would seem like an appropriate tune with which to welcome the
pianist to the bandstand.

Hal Gaylor has been identified in various sources as the bassist after the intermission.
However, participating musicians, including Bobby Malloy and Bill Graham, remember Bob
Rudd playing the second set. This is substantiated by Dobbin's notes. Also contrary to pub-
lished sources, Dick Garcia is present, albeit no more than faintly audible, on *Embraceable
You*. He does not solo.

Dobbin's notes indicate the Parker sets were the fifth and seventh of the afternoon.
Nothing survives, or is known, of the sixth.

III/MASSEY HALL
178 Victoria St., Toronto, 15 May 1953, 8:30-11:30 p.m.

CBC All-Stars: Graham Topping (tpt, leader), Don Johnson, Julius
Piekarz, Bernie Rowe, Erich Traugott (tpts), Ross Culley, Ron
Hughes, Russ Meyers, Steve Richards (trbs), Gordie Evans (as),
Bernie Piltch (as), Julian Filanowski (ts), Hart Wheeler (ts), Norman
Symonds (bs), Ralph Fraser (p), Howie Morris (b), Doug Bennett (d)

The Goof and I	unissued
Why Do I Love You?	unissued
All the Things You Are	unissued
Harvard Blues	unissued
Mambo	unissued
Beaver Junction	unissued
The Nearness of You	unissued

Fugue for Reeds and Brass   unissued

What's Shmoo?   unissued

Elevation   unissued

Dizzy Gillespie (tpt), Charlie Parker (as), Bud Powell (p), Charles
Mingus (b), Max Roach (d)
[titles listed in sequence of original release, probably an accurate
representation of the concert]
    Perdido   Debut DLP2/DEB 124*

    Salt Peanuts (DG/CP vocal)   Debut DLP2/DEB 124

    All the Things You Are/52nd
    Street Theme   Debut DLP2/DEB 124

Roach
    Drum Conversation   Design DLP29/Gala GLP 328/
                                       Allegro ALL 773

add Powell, Mingus
[tunes listed in sequence of original release, probably not an accurate representation of the concert]
    Cherokee   Debut DLP3

    Embraceable You   Debut DLP3

    Jubilee   Debut DLP3

    Sure Thing   Debut DLP3

    [*Bass-ically Speaking*   Debut DLP3]**

    Lullaby of Birdland   Debut DLP3

I've Got You Under My Skin   Debut DLP198

add Parker, Gillespie
[titles listed in sequence of original release]
   Wee   Debut DLP4/DEB 124

   Hot House   Debut DLP4/DEB 124

   A Night in Tunisia   Debut DLP4/DEB 124

CBC All-Stars: as before
   Lover Come Back to Me   unissued

   Just Where You Are   unissued

   Mambo Macocoa   unissued

add Parker, Gillespie, Mingus, Roach
   unknown title, [*Tiny's Blues?*]   recorded?

---

*Debut DLP2, DLP3 and DLP4 were 10" albums, released successively as volumes 1, 2 and 3 of *Jazz at Massey Hall*, the first two by the end of 1953 and the third early in 1954.

   [Mingus' overdubbed bass can be heard on all of DLP4 save for his solo on *Hot House* which survives intact through all issues.]

   In view of his contract with Mercury Records, Parker was identified by Debut as "Charlie Chan," a play on both his wife's name and that of the popular movie character from the 1930s and 40s. The Massey Hall tapes had in fact been offered to Mercury's Norman Granz for a reported $100,000. Granz declined.

   Debut DEB124 was a 12" release combining the quintet albums DLP2 and DLP4; it was also titled *Jazz at Massey Hall* and was subsequently reissued by Fantasy (86003).

   [Mingus' overdubbed bass has now been added to *Perdido* and *All the Things You Are*, but not *Salt Peanuts*, which survives in its original form through all issues.]

   The Powell trio's Debut DLP3, together with four tracks of Powell with George Duvivier (bass) and Art Taylor (drums) dated to September of 1953, was issued in 12" form as *Jazz at Massey Hall, Volume Two/Trio... the Amazing Bud Powell*. It retained the catalogue number DLP3.

   The Powell trio's *I've Got You Under My Skin* from Massey Hall was first issued on Debut DEB198, *Autobiography in Jazz*, a sampler of the label's artists. *I've Got You Under My Skin* replaced *Bass-ically Speaking* when the 12" DLP3 was repackaged in 1962 by Fantasy as *The Bud Powell Trio* (86006).

Fantasy again reissued the 12" DLP3 (without the substitution for *Bass-ically Speaking*) in 1984 as part of its Original Jazz Classics series (OJC-111).

Prestige Records repackaged Fantasy 86003 (ie. the six quintet tracks) in 1973 with Fantasy 86006 (ie. six trio tracks from Massey Hall plus the four Duvivier/Taylor performances) as *The Greatest Jazz Concert Ever* (PR24024).

The trio set has also been issued in whole or in part in England by Vogue and in Denmark by Debut. The quintet tracks have also been released together or individually, and in original or overdubbed form, under various labels in various countries, including England (Vogue, Design, Gala, Allegro and Saga), France (Vogue, Swing and America), Sweden (Spectrum, Jazz Selections), Denmark (Debut), Germany (Brunswick), Italy (Jam Session) and Japan (Debut).

** As released on Debut DLP3, both 10" and 12", *Bass-ically Speaking* is a studio recording from the same period with Billy Taylor at the piano. It has been presumed that a version of the piece was also played at Massey Hall.

Bibliography

Barris, Alex. "The Record Album," *The Globe and Mail* (6 Feb 1953)

——. "Home talent holds own with U.S. jazz stars," *The Globe and Mail* (18 May 1953)

Batten, Jack, Brown, Don & Hare, Alan E. Letters to the editor, *Jazz Journal* (May 1970)

Batten, Jack. "Where was the greatest jazz concert ever? In Toronto of all places," *Saturday Night* (May 1978)

Callaghan, Morley, *The Loved and the Lost* (Toronto 1951)

Coss, Bill. Liner notes, *Jazz at Massey Hall* (Debut DEB 124) [reprinted in *The Jazz Word*, Cerulli, Dom *et al* eds. (New York 1960)]

Dobbin, Len. "Final bar" [Bob Rudd], *Coda* (December 1971)

——. "33 years ago, jazz history was being made in Montreal," *The Gazette* (6 Feb 1985)

Giddins, Gary. *Celebrating Bird: The Triumph of Charlie Parker* (New York 1987)

Gillespie, Dizzy & Fraser, Al. *To Be or Not to Bop* (Garden City, NY, 1979)

Gilmore, John. *Swinging in Paradise* (Montreal 1988)

Gitler, Ira. *Jazz Masters of the Forties* (New York 1966)

Goddard, Peter. "Date to remember in history of jazz," *Toronto Star* (14 May 1978)

Hennessey, Mike. "Charles Mingus: changed man?" *Down Beat* (13 May 1971)

James, Michael. "Jazz at Massey Hall," *Jazz Monthly* (February 1963)

Johnstone, Ken. "How Plante and Drapeau licked the Montreal underworld," *Maclean's Magazine* (1 December 1954)

Koch, Lawrence O. *Yardbird Suite: A Compendium of the Music & Life of Charlie Parker* (Bowling Green, Ohio, 1988)

Litchfield, Jack. *The Canadian Jazz Discography 1916-1980* (Toronto 1982)

Lyons, Len. "Paul Bley: improvising artist," *Contemporary Keyboard* (May 1977)

McRae, Barry. *Dizzy Gillespie* (Tunbridge Wells, Kent, England, 1988)

Miller, Mark. *Boogie, Pete & the Senator* (Toronto 1987)

Parker, Chan & Paudras, Francis. *To Bird with Love* (Antigny,

France, 1980)

Peterson, Owen. "The Massey Hall Concert," *Jazz Journal* (March 1970)

Priestley, Brian. *Mingus: A Critical Biography* (London 1982)

——. *Charlie Parker* (Tunbridge Wells, Kent, England, 1984)

Reisner, Robert. *Bird: The Legend of Charlie Parker* (New York 1962)

Russell, Ross. *Bird Lives!* (New York 1973)

Saks, Norman, Bukowski, Leonard & Bregman, Robert M. *Yardbird Inc: The Charlie Parker Discography* (New York 1989) [published privately]

Scharf, Alan. Letter to the editor, *Saturday Night* (September 1978)

White, Keith. *Noting the Scene* (Montreal, no date) [unpublished manuscript]

Index

Alberta Lounge (Montreal) 27
All the Things You Are 83, 88, 104, 105
Allen's Alley (Wee) 88
American Federation of Musicians 97
Anka, Paul 49
Arabia, Phil 30, 32
Armstrong, Louis 23, 67
Automatistes 26

Baculis, Al 42
Baird, Carlton 49
Balanchine, George 32
Bandbox (New York) 18, 29, 55
Barker, Danny 71fn
Barris, Alex 63, 64, 66, 67, 68, 73, 95
Basie, Count 75
Bass-ically Speaking 87fn, 104, 106fn
Basso, Guido 52
Battagello, Walter 52
Batten, Jack 10, 59, 85, 93
Beaver Café (Montreal) 39
Beaver Junction 75, 103
Beliveau, Jean 23
Belmont Park (Montreal) 99
Beneath the Underdog (Mingus) 62
Bennett, Doug 74, 103
Berkley, Laura 36, 37
Berman, Morton 98
Bernie's Tune 37, 44, 101
Berry, Chu 71fn
Best, Denzil 88
Bird Lives! (Russell) 20
Bird of Paradise 83, 84
Birdland (New York) 18, 57, 68, 69
Birks Works 81
Biss, Harry 97, 98
Blakey, Art 100
Bley, Paul (Buzzy) 9-10, 26, 27-32, 34, 35, 37, 38, 39, 41, 42, 43, 47, 52, 53, 61, 99-100, 101
Blue Note (Records) 18
Borduas, Paul-Émile 26
Brooklyn Dodgers 26
Byrd, Emry 49

Café St-Michel (Montreal) 25, 49
Callaghan, Morley 24, 25
Callender, Red 33
Calloway, Cab 71fn

Cameron, Don 33-39, 44-45, 51, 101
Canadian All Stars 42
Canadian Ambassadors (Mynie Sutton's) 48
Canadian Jazz Discography 1916-1980 (Litchfield) 9
Candido 100
Candoli, Pete 99
Carmen 89
Carmen, Perry 33
Caron, Justice François 24
The Casino (Toronto) 69fn
Catlett, Sid 48
Cavendish Café (Montreal) 100
CBC All-Stars 66, 68, 74, 103, 104, 105
Chan, Charlie 93, 105fn
Cherokee 86, 104
Chez Paree 7, 18, 19, 23, 28, 29, 30, 31, 33, 37, 42-51, 52, 99
Christy, June 100
Clarke, Kenny 69
Cluesman, Leo 98
Coda (Toronto) 39
Cole, Cozy 71fn
Colonial Tavern (Toronto) 57, 58, 71, 73
Cool Blues 35-36, 47, 101, 102, 103fn
Coss, Bill 9, 62fn, 70
Cowans, Al 25
Culley, Ross 74, 75, 103

Dameron, Tadd 89, 90
Davis, Stephen 9
Debut Records 9, 62fn, 65, 70, 87, 100, 104-105, 106fn
Delta Rhythm Boys 33
Dial Records 17, 35, 36, 37, 46, 50
Discovery (Records) 42
Dobbin, Len 10, 39, 41, 102, 103
Dolphy, Eric 89
Domino (Montreal) 52
Don't Blame Me 37-38, 102
Donahue, Sam 75
Douglas, Tommy 16
Down Beat (Chicago) 32, 62fn, 64, 78, 99
Downbeat, The (Montreal) 36
Drapeau, Jean 24
Drum Conversation 85, 86, 104
Dutton, Gary 59, 85
Duvivier, George 105fn, 106fn

Eager, Allen 88, 99
Eckstine, Billy 17
Eldridge, Roy 81

Elektra Musician (Records) 18
Elevation 75, 104
Ellington, Duke 62, 64, 65, 73
Emanon Jazz Society (Montreal) 28, 34, 39, 40, 42, 43, 49, 52, 99
Embraceable You 47, 50, 87, 102, 103fn, 104
Ensemble de musique improvisée de Montréal 26
Evans, Gordie 71, 74, 75, 76, 77, 84-85, 91, 92, 103

Farnon, Robert 71fn
Feather, Roger 61, 93
Festival International de Jazz de Montréal 31
Festival of Modern Jazz 100
52nd Street Theme 84, 91, 104
Filanowski, Julian 74, 75, 76, 91, 92, 103
The Firebird 32
First Annual Festival of Creative Jazz (Massey Hall) 59, 63, 67
Fleet, Biddy 16
Fleming, Gordie 42
Ford Hotel (Montreal) 32
Ford Hotel (Toronto) 71
Fraser, Ralph 74, 76, 91, 92, 103
Fugue for Reeds and Brass 75, 104
Fulford, Robert 64

Gale Agency (Moe) 62, 65
Garcia, Dick 8, 30-31, 32, 35, 37, 38, 39, 42, 44, 46, 47, 49, 50, 51, 99, 101, 102, 103fn
Garner, Erroll 17, 100
Gaylor, Hal 27, 33, 42, 43, 44, 45, 48, 102, 103fn
Gazette (Montreal) 30, 31, 39
Gershwin, George 35, 50, 87
Getz, Stan 57, 58
Gillespie, Dizzy 7, 9, 16, 18, 52, 55, 58, 59, 62, 63, 64, 65, 67, 69, 70, 71, 78-79, 80-81, 82, 83, 84-85, 88, 89, 90, 91, 92, 93, 95, 100, 104, 105, 108
Gilmore, John 25
Girard, Willy 25
Gitler, Ira 65
The Globe and Mail (Toronto) 17, 58, 59, 63, 66, 68, 73, 95, 100
Goddard, Peter 10, 69fn
Goodman, Benny 67
Goodstein, Oscar 69, 70, 71, 86
The Goof and I 75, 103
Gordons, The 66
Grafton (musical instruments) 20-21, 34

Graham, Bill 27, 31, 42, 43, 45, 46, 50, 53, 102, 103fn
Granatstein, Art 58, 60, 61, 62-63, 67
Grand Prix du Disque 36
Granz, Norman 105fn
Grimes, Tiny 16
Guild Records 16, 82, 89

Haig, Al 100
Hakala Café (Montreal) 100
Hambourg, Clem 57
Hambourg, Ruth 57
Hampton, Lionel 57, 73
Happy Gang 71fn
Harris, Benny 38, 97
Harris-Jackson Herd 55
Hartnett Music Studios (New York) 30-31, 60, 61
Harvard Blues 75, 103
Hennessey, Mike 62fn, 93
Henry, Conrad 97
Her Majesty's Theatre (Montreal) 23, 25
Herald (Montreal) 30, 31, 40, 97
Herman, Woody 64, 68, 75
Hines, Earl 17, 57, 97, 98
Hoare, Bill 61
Hodges, Johnny 97, 98
Hot House 89, 90fn, 93, 105
Houde, Camillien 23
House of Hambourg (Toronto) 57, 58
Household Finance 63
How High the Moon 45, 46
Howard Theatre (Washington) 18
Hughes, Ron 74, 103

I've Got You Under My Skin 87, 105
In An English Country Garden 50
International Band (Louis Metcalf's) 25, 26, 49

Jackson, Cal 56, 63, 66, 68
James, Harry 52
Jazz Artists Club (Toronto) 57
Jazz at the Philharmonic 58, 77, 80, 81
"Jazz by Jackson" (CBC TV) 56, 63
Jazz Journal 9, 20
Jazz Masters of the Forties (Gitler) 65
The Jazz Review, 71fn
"Jazz Unlimited" (CBC Radio) 56, 63, 65, 66
Jazz Workshop 7, 8, 9, 10, 26, 27-28, 29, 30, 31, 32, 33, 39, 40, 43, 48, 51-52, 99-100
"Jazz Workshop" (CBFT) 29, 30, 31, 33-39, 56, 100, 101, 102

Johann Sebastian Bop 35, 101
Johnson, Don 74, 103
Johnson, J.J. 59
Jones, Jimmy 48
Jones, Jo 16
Jordan, Buddy 25
Joss, Bert 42, 44, 46-47, 48, 49, 51, 102fn, 103fn
Jubilee 86, 104
Jumpin' with Symphony Sid 34, 101
Just Where You Are 91, 105

Kahn, Tiny 92
Kavakos Grill (Washington) 18, 20
Kennedy, George 27
Kenney, Mart 68
Kenton, Stan 100
Kern, Jerome 83, 88
The Kerry Dance, 83
King Edward Hotel (Toronto) 85
Konitz, Lee 100

Landry, Yvan 27, 42, 43, 46
Langlois, Bob 52
Latin Quarter (Montreal) 39, 52-53, 97-98
Laura 80-81, 89
Lauzon, Willie 40-41, 42
Lavallée, Roland 33
Lee, Peggy 99
Lewis, John 69
Life (New York) 78
Lindsay's (Montreal) 27, 39, 51, 58
Litchfield, Jack 9, 102fn
Louis, Benny 99
The Loved and the Lost (Callaghan) 24, 26
Lover Come Back to Me 91, 105
Lullaby of Birdland 86, 104
Lundy, B.T. 25
Lymburner, John 28
Lyons, Len 10, 29

Machito 17
Maini, Joe 28, 29
Maison Doré (Toronto) 57
Malloy, Bobby 49-50, 102, 103fn
Mambo 75, 103
Mambo Macocoa 91, 105
Marciano, Rocky 33, 66, 68, 84
Mardigan, Art 97
Maroon Club (Montreal) 30
Massey Hall (Toronto) 7, 8, 9, 10, 17, 18, 20-21, 55, 56, 57, 58, 60, 61, 62fn, 65, 66,

67, 68, 70, 71, 72-93, 95, 100, 103
McDougall, Dick 67, 68
McHugh, Jimmy 38
McKay, Cliff 56
McLean, Jackie 99
McNamara, Helen 57, 64, 68
"McNamara's Bandwagon" 64, 65, 68
McRae, Barry 9
McShann, Jay 17, 36
Menuhin, Yehudi 23
Mercure, Pierre 33
Mercury (Records) 46, 94, 105fn
Meredith, Russ 39
Metcalf, Louis 25, 26
Metronome (New York) 20, 32-33, 87, 94, 95
Meyers, Russ 74, 91, 103
Michaud, Neil 9, 27, 30, 32, 34, 35, 38, 39, 43, 44, 101
"Michel", Neil 9
Miller, Bernie 37
Mingus, Celia 69, 70
Mingus, Charles 7, 8, 9, 18, 55, 58, 62, 64-66, 69, 70, 71, 72-73, 79fn, 80, 83, 84, 85, 86, 87, 89-90, 91, 92-93, 94, 95, 100, 104-105
Monk, Thelonious 16
Montreal Royals 25-26
Moore, Brew 8, 30, 37, 38, 39, 40, 42, 44, 52, 80, 99, 101, 102
Moose the Mooche 49, 102, 103fn
Morris, Howie 74, 77, 103
Most, Sam 99
Mulligan, Gerry 30, 37, 75

National Film Board 59
The Nearness of You, 75, 103
New Jazz Society (NJS) 7, 31, 55, 58-63, 64, 65, 66, 67, 68, 71, 72, 86, 93, 94, 95, 100
New York City Ballet 32
A Night in Tunisia 79, 90, 91, 105
Niosi, Bert 56
Noble, Ray 86
Norvo, Red 71
Now's the Time 51, 102

O'Reilly, Ted 64, 72-73, 79fn, 87
On the Trail 83
Orchestra, The 20, 55
Orgen, The (Montreal) 44, 49
Ornithology 46, 53, 102

Park Plaza Hotel (Toronto) 57
Parker, Addie 16

Parker, Chan 69
Parker, Charles Sr. 16
Parker, Charlie 7-10, 15-21, 23, 24, 28-33, 34-39, 40-42, 43-48, 49-51, 52-53, 55-56, 57, 58, 59, 60, 61-63, 64, 65, 68-70, 71, 72, 75, 78-85, 88-95, 97-98, 100, 101-105
Parker, Pree 18, 19
Paskert, Ted 9, 32, 35, 38, 39, 42, 99, 101
"Pastor", Ted 9
Patton, Stan 68
Pearce, Pat 30, 32
Perdido 38, 79, 79fn, 84, 102, 104, 105fn
Peterson, Oscar 7, 27, 32, 49
Pettiford, Oscar 58, 64-65
Piekarz, Julius 74, 91, 103
Piltch, Bernie 74, 76, 103
Plante, Pacifique (Pax) 24
Porter, Cole 87
Powell, Bud 7, 8, 18, 49, 55, 59, 62, 63, 64, 65, 69, 70, 71, 72, 80, 81, 82, 83, 84, 85-88, 89, 90, 91, 95, 104-105
Powell, Carrie 16
Powell, Mel 99
Premier Radio (Toronto) 57, 95
Priestley, Brian 9

Raeburn, Boyd 59, 72, 94
Rajotte, Huguette 40-42, 47
Rand, Sally 39
"The Record Album" (*Globe and Mail*) 63, 67
Refus global 26
Richards, Steve 74, 79, 103
Rico, Joe 57
Roach, Max 7, 18, 20, 46, 55, 58, 62, 63, 64, 65, 66, 70, 71, 74, 79, 80, 81, 82, 84, 85, 86, 87, 88, 89, 90, 91, 92, 93, 95, 104-105
Roberts, Art 98
Robinson, Harold 21
Robinson, Jackie 26
Roby, Bob 27, 31, 32
Rockhead's Paradise (Montreal) 25
Rollins, Sonny 26, 99
Rowe, Bernie 74, 75, 103
Royal Winnipeg Ballet 59
Royal York Hotel (Toronto) 94
Rudd, Bob 8, 33, 48, 49, 53, 102, 103fn
Russell, Curley 69
Russell, Ross 9, 20

's Wonderful 35, 101
Salt Peanuts 81-82, 83, 84, 88, 89, 104, 105fn
Saturday Night (Toronto) 85, 94
Savoy Records 16, 17, 50, 85
Scharf, Alan 72, 86, 92-93, 94-95
Seville Theatre (Montreal) 23, 25
Shearing, George 28, 30, 57, 58, 86, 87
Silver Rail (Toronto) 57, 72, 84, 88
Sinatra, Frank 23, 42, 44
Sissle, Noble 48
Smith, Buster 16
Smith, Roy 56, 75, 91
Soundscription Service (Montreal) 42
Spanier, Herbie 99, 100
Speight Soundcraft Laboratories 75
Speight, Norm 75
St. Moritz Roof (Montreal) 30, 39
Standard (Montreal) 26
Daily Star (Toronto) 68
Stewart, Slam 17
Storyville (Boston) 18
Sure Thing 87-88, 104
Sutton, Mynie 48
Swinging in Paradise (Gilmore) 25
Symonds, Norman 68, 74, 75, 76, 103

Taft Hotel (New York) 61
Tatum, Art 16, 87
Taylor, Art 99, 105fn
Taylor, Billy 106fn
Telegram (Toronto) 57, 64, 65, 68
"1010 Swing Club" (CBC Radio) 56, 65, 67
Thompson, Lucky 48
Thornhill, Claude 30, 32
Tiny's Blues 92, 105
Tizol, Juan 38, 62, 79
To Be or Not to Bop (Gillespie) 64, 79
To Bird with Love (Parker/Paudras) 55. 98
Topping, Graham 56, 66, 67-68, 71, 73-77, 79, 91-92, 93, 95, 103
Torin, Symphony Sid 34
Tormé, Mel 57
Toronto Symphony Orchestra 65
Toth, Jerry 75
Tramp Band (Al Cowan's) 25
Traugott, Erich 71, 73-74, 77, 78, 103
Tristano, Lennie 58, 59

Ulanov, Barry 94

United Jewish People's Order Hall (Toronto)
  58

Vaughan, Sarah 59
Video Café (Montreal) 28, 39, 40, 51, 52, 99
Vogel, Vic 51-52

Wade, Alfie Jr. 28, 43-44
Wade, Harold (Steep) 8, 24, 25, 26, 44, 45, 48-
  51, 102, 103fn
Wahoo 38, 80, 97, 102
Walcott, Jersey Joe 33, 66, 68, 84, 88
Ware, Efferge 16
Watanabe, Jiro (Butch) 25
Waters, Ethel 57
Wattam, Dick 55, 58-60, 61, 63, 65-66, 68,
  69-70, 72, 86, 93-94, 95
Wayne, Chuck 28
Wayne, Max 99
Wee 88, 89, 105
Wellman, Allen 33
West, Harold (Doc) 17
What's Shmoo? 75, 104
Wheeler, Hart 68, 74, 75-77, 91, 92, 103
Whiston, Henry 99
White, Keith 27, 34, 42-43, 47-48,102fn
Why Do I Love You? 103
Wilkinson, Mark (Wilkie) 25, 49
Williams, Floyd 27
Williams, Valdo 8, 27, 33, 45-46, 47, 102
Wilson, Earl 78
Wilson, Gerald 48
Winding, Kai 30, 99

Young, Lester 34, 37
Young, Trummy 17

About the author...

Mark Miller has been the jazz critic for *The Globe and Mail*
(Toronto) since 1978 and is a contributor to *down beat* (Chicago)
and *Jazz Forum* (Warsaw). His previous books are *Jazz in Canada:
Fourteen Lives* (Toronto 1982) and *Boogie, Pete & the Senator*
(Toronto 1987).

About the photographers...

Harold Robinson, a news photographer for *The Globe and Mail* in
1953, was engaged by the New Jazz Society to shoot the Massey
Hall concert. Two of his 12 photographs appeared without credit in
Metronome in August 1953; at least six different Robinson shots
from the concert have since been published, again without proper
credit, in books about Parker, Gillespie and Mingus, as well as in
magazines and on record covers. In most cases credit, if given at all,
has gone to private collectors in the USA or Europe. Robinson, who
died in 1981, was apparently never paid for the original assignment,
nor for the subsequent, uncredited use of his photographs.

Alan Scharf was a member of the New Jazz Society in 1953. An
engineer by profession, he now operates a consulting company in
Saskatoon. His photographs from Massey Hall are published here
for the first time.

Huguette (Rajotte) Schwartz was a member of the Emanon Jazz
Society in 1953. Mme Schwartz works now in the tourism industry
in Montreal. Her photograph of Charlie Parker at the Chez Paree is
published here for the first time.